HOW

Study the
BIBLE

James Braga

MULTNOMAH
Portland, Oregon 97266

Foreign language editions of *How to Study the Bible* are in print for:

Indonesian (Penerbit Gandum Mas, Malang, Indonesia)
Spanish (Life Publishers, Miami, Florida)
French (Life Publishers, Miami, Florida)
Portuguese (Life Publishers, Miami, Florida)
Chinese (Christian Communications Ltd, Hong Kong)

Unless otherwise identified, all Scripture quotations are from the Holy Bible: New International Version, copyright 1978 by the International Bible Society. Used by permission of Zondervan Bible Publishers.

Scripture quotations marked NASB are from the New American Standard Bible, © The Lockman Foundation 1960, 1962, 1963, 1968, 1971, 1972, 1973, 1975, 1977. Used by permission.

Scripture quotations marked KJV are from the King James Version of the Bible.

HOW TO STUDY THE BIBLE
© 1982 by Multnomah Press
Portland, Oregon 97266

Printed in the United States of America

All rights reserved. No part of this publication may be reproduced, stored in a retrieval system, or transmitted, in any form or by any means, electronic, mechanical, photocopying, recording, or otherwise, without the prior written permission of the publisher.

Library of Congress Cataloging-in-Publication Data

Braga, James
  How to study the Bible.
  Bibliography: p.
  1. Bible—Study.   I. Title
BS600.2.B69   220'.07   82-6420
ISBN 0-930014-72-3 (pbk.)   AACR2

93   94   95   -   10   9   8   7   6   5

*To the Christian
who desires to know the Lord Jesus Christ better
by the study of His Word.*

CONTENTS

INTRODUCTION

One of the greatest privileges that God has given to His children is the opportunity to study His Word. Most Christians would agree that this, indeed, is a true statement. Yet too many of us today do not give ourselves to real Bible study; we are content instead to be spoon-fed, to receive our spiritual nourishment second hand. We know little of the experience of the prophet who wrote, "Thy words were found and I ate them, and Thy words became for me a joy and the delight of my heart; for I have been called by Thy name, O LORD God of hosts" (Jeremiah 15:16 NASB).

Perhaps one of the reasons so many fail in Bible study is that they simply do not know how to go about it. If you fear you will fail, I have prepared for that event with the simple skills and guidance found in the chapters of this book. Each chapter is an approach to studying a single book of the Bible, proven to work in an easy "do-it-yourself" way. Whether it is a long book or a short one, a narrative or a letter, the methods in these chapters will guide you to vital, living truths you will discover for yourself.

There is one prerequisite to all that I have said, however. Reading any book of the Bible prayerfully, numerous times, under the guidance of the Holy Spirit is an absolute must for success in understanding the Scriptures. Heed the call of Joshua 1:8—"Do not let this Book of the Law depart from your mouth; meditate on it day and night, so that you may be careful to do everything written in it. Then you will be prosperous and successful." Jesus Christ said, "He [the Holy Spirit] will guide you into all truth" (John 16:13). And in confident prayer we can expect with the psalmist fruitful reward from the study: "Open my eyes that I may see wonderful things in your law" (Psalm 119:18).

Before you begin your study, I have two suggestions. First, each chapter ends with an exercise that you must perform on your own. It is designed to enable you to learn by doing what you have been taught in the chapter. I have placed the answers to the exercises at the end of the book so that you can check each assignment with my work after you have completed your own.

The second suggestion concerns Bible translations and reference books. The King James Version of the Bible is a good translation; in addition to it, you should also have a copy of at least one of the modern translations. Both the New American Standard Bible and the New International Version of the Bible are widely used and appreciated. A parallel translation of the New Testament—a book which places several Bible translations side-by-side in parallel columns—is also very helpful. Avoid using a paraphrase of the Bible for Bible study. It is limited in that it is a thought-for-word translation, and accurate Bible study focuses on each individual word of the text.

Reference books you will later want include an unabridged concordance (a book that lists every location of important biblical words), a Bible atlas, and a good Bible dictionary or encyclopedia. Pen, paper, and a looseleaf notebook complete your list of tools for studying a book in the Bible.

This book is designed to be simple, but capable of equipping its reader to understand the basic truths of biblical books. It is concise, but in step-by-step fashion it never assumes that details are not important and necessary for thorough understanding of Bible study methods. In fact, I have made only one assumption throughout the book—you can learn to study a book in the Bible.

1. THE SYNTHETIC APPROACH:

Discovering the Divisions

Down through the ages many of the world's greatest thinkers and scholars have grappled with the truths of the Bible. And yet at the same time, individuals with very little schooling or training have derived the highest benefits from the study of its pages.

Devout scholars have sought by every possible means to unlock the Bible's treasures and to devise means of discovering its secrets. But no matter what methods men have used to study the sixty-six books which comprise the divine library, no one has ever been able to plumb its depths or to exhaust its contents. So today, as always, this supernatural Book presents a challenge to every earnest believer to search its contents and to discover anew its timeless truths.

By the grace of God, it is possible to obtain a good measure of knowledge of His Word, and there are certain well-defined procedures which may be followed to gain this end.

This book seeks to present several approaches to the study of a book in the Bible which will help you learn to study the Bible on your own. To begin, we will learn how to obtain an overview of a book using the synthetic approach.

Definition of the Synthetic Method

The word synthesis means "to place or put together" various parts or elements to make up a whole. That will be our goal in doing a synthetic study of a book in the Bible—to get a graphic view of the book as a whole as a result of noting its main parts and their relationship to each other and to the whole. By studying the book synthetically, we will learn to follow the main trend of thought from beginning to end and thus be able to think our way through the book.

The portion of Scripture we have selected for synthetic study is the

11

book of Jonah. As we begin our study, it would be helpful to turn now to the book of Jonah and read through its four chapters several times. If you are to learn the book and have a grasp of its contents and message, you can only do so by prayerful and repeated reading of its four chapters.

Qualities of an Effective Synthetic Chart

The first step in our study is the construction of a synthetic chart. Such a chart will help us gain that overview that is the goal of the synthetic approach to Bible study. Here are several qualities that will help to make the chart effective:

1. Clarity.
Everything in the chart should be understandable at a glance.

2. Brevity.
The chart should not contain long involved sentences or ideas. Each thought should be expressed as concisely as possible. Most items can be stated in a simple phrase—or even a single word.

3. Relevancy.
All the material in the chart should be derived only from the book you are studying. For example, if your chart is on the book of Exodus, you will not bring into it something on the gospel of John, or if your study is Ephesians, you will not make reference to the book of Revelation.

4. Intelligibility.
This simply means that your chart should be understandable—so understandable that if you were to come back to your work a year or two later you would be able to comprehend it immediately.

5. Simplicity.
The chart should not be complicated or cluttered with too many ideas. This is a common error. The tendency is to fill the chart with a conglomeration of words instead of making it simple, clear, and to the point.

6. Comprehensiveness.

Your aim should be to synthesize the contents of the book. There are obviously many, many details even in a brief book in the Bible, but to synthesize a book you must avoid particularizing items. Record only material which is significant as well as inclusive.

7. Neatness

A "clean" chart will always be easier to follow than one which is filled with blots, scratches, and corrections.

Basic Steps in the Construction of a Synthetic Chart of a Book in the Bible

We are now ready to begin the construction of a synthetic chart on the book of Jonah. Be sure to have your Bible open to the book of Jonah so that you can read the text at every point that we indicate. Only after reading the text will you be able to see the necessity for each step in the construction of the chart.

Step 1—A Chart with Diagonal Lines

Prepare an adequate number of diagonal spaces to record the summary of each paragraph or chapter in the book.

This is done by taking a sheet of 8½" by 11" paper and placing it horizontally on the desk. Draw a horizontal line across the center of the page. Leading from the horizontal line, at an angle of about 75 degrees, draw a series of diagonal lines with a space of about one inch between each diagonal line. Above the diagonal lines write the name of the book you are studying.

As we will see later, each space between the diagonal lines allows for the summary of a paragraph or chapter in a book. Of course, the more chapters or paragraphs there are in a book, the more diagonal spaces required. According to our divisions, there are eleven paragraphs in the book of Jonah and we have drawn twelve diagonal lines to provide eleven spaces. (See Figure 1.)

Step 2—Summarizing the Paragraphs

Summarize in a brief phrase the contents of each paragraph or chapter in the book and use the space between the diagonal lines to record your summary. In the lower left-hand corner of each diagonal

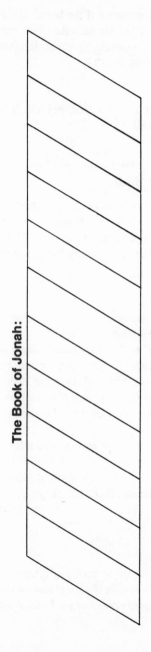

Figure 1

space, state the reference (by chapter and verse) with which each paragraph or chapter begins.

Turn to Jonah 1:1-3 and consider these verses carefully. Try to sum them up in a brief phrase of eight words or less. Write your summary of these verses in the first space between the first two diagonal lines. In the lower left-hand corner of that space write "1:1." This indicates that the first paragraph on your chart begins at chapter 1, verse 1.

If you have followed these instructions thoroughly, you now have your own summary of the first paragraph. One possible summary of these verses is: Disobedience of Jonah to commission. Your summary may be worded differently, but it should indicate the main idea of the paragraph.

At this point we must add a few details to Step 2.

Addition to Step 2—"Parallel Thoughts for Paragraph Summaries"

Summaries of paragraphs or chapters should be in parallel structure; that is, they should be matched or balanced with each other. For example, if the summary of the first paragraph consists of three or four words, the second paragraph should not be nine or ten words in length. Also, when the summary of the first paragraph begins with a noun, the rest of the summaries should begin with a noun or a participle, which is a verbal noun. In order to qualify a noun, it is often suitable for the article and an adjective to precede it.

Additionally, the paragraph summaries should be expressed in the same tense. If the summary of one paragraph is stated in the present tense the others should also be expressed in the present tense.

Now let us proceed with the second paragraph, Jonah 1:4-9. Carefully read these verses, write your own paragraph summary, and record your summary in the second diagonal space. In the lower left-hand corner of the space write "1:4." This indicates that the second paragraph begins at chapter 1, verse 4. It also means that the summary of your first paragraph ends just before the verse where the second paragraph begins, or at verse 3. Because of the cramped space between the diagonal lines, we write "1:1" instead of "1:1-3."

Complete your summary of each of the successive paragraphs: 1:10-14; 1:15-16; 1:17-2:9; 2:10; 3:1-4; 3:5-9; 3:10-4:4; 4:5-8; and 4:9-11.

The chapter divisions in our Bibles are not always accurate guides to the breaks in the thought of the writer. So we should not always construct our charts according to these chapter divisions. We find this to be true with the fifth paragraph in the book of Jonah. This paragraph does not actually begin at the first verse of chapter 2, but rather at 1:17. Also, the thought of chapter 4:1-4 actually begins at 3:10. Now note Figure 2 showing the summary of each paragraph in Jonah. Observe also how these summaries are balanced or mated with each other.

You may be wondering what you should do if you were studying a book with only five or six chapters but which nevertheless has twenty-five, thirty, or forty paragraphs, or with a book which contains a large number of chapters. How would we then manage to make a chart summarizing every one of these chapters or paragraphs? To meet this problem, take note of the following elaboration of Step 2.

Addition to Step 2—"Too Many Paragraphs, Too Many Chapters"

If it is a short book which has too many paragraphs, simply combine such successive paragraphs whose concepts are so closely related to one another or whose contents are so similar as to allow them to be treated as a unit, and make one paragraph out of two or more successive paragraphs. If a book has too many chapters, follow the same procedure by combining the successive chapters which are closely related to one another and summarize that block of chapters as one section.

With our synthetic chart on Jonah, each paragraph generally contains a single topic. But this is not always the case. This is illustrated in the second paragraph where we have two topics: the storm and the discovery of the man who was the cause of it. If it had been necessary, we could have extended our chart by giving two separate diagonal spaces to cover these two items, but we avoided doing this in order to follow our paragraph divisions. (See Figure 2.)

Step 3—Selecting the Main Divisions

Note the successive paragraphs or chapters which have a common topic or which are in some way closely related to one another and combine them to form the main divisions of the book. Give a suitable title to each main division of the book and indicate the chapters and verses covering each main division. These main divisions provide the basic outline or structure of the book.

Show the main divisions directly below the diagonal lines of the chart. The titles of the main divisions should be parallel in structure; that is, they should be matched or balanced with one another.

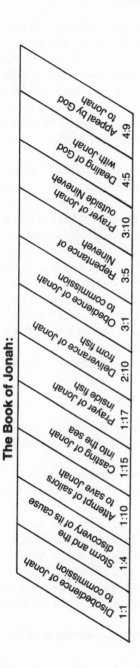

The Book of Jonah:

1:1	Disobedience of Jonah to commission
1:4	Storm and the discovery of its cause
1:10	Attempt of sailors to save Jonah
1:15	Casting of Jonah into the sea
1:17	Prayer of Jonah inside fish
2:10	Deliverance of Jonah from fish
3:1	Obedience of Jonah to commission
3:5	Repentance of Nineveh
3:10	Prayer of Jonah outside Nineveh
4:5	Dealing of God with Jonah
4:9	Appeal by God to Jonah

Figure 2

As we think over the four chapters in the book of Jonah, we note that the first chapter tells us about Jonah's first commission to go to Nineveh and the consequences of his disobedience. From 1:17 through 2:9, we read of the prophet's experience inside the fish and his remarkable prayer. When we reach 3:1, we read that "the word of the Lord came to Jonah a second time," followed by the account of Jonah's obedience and the astounding results that followed his ministry in Nineveh. Following this, there is an obvious break in the account.

It is plainly evident that all the paragraphs which precede 3:1 are related in one way or another to the first commission God gave to Jonah, and, beginning at 3:1 to the end of the book, all the paragraphs in this section are related to Jonah's second commission. We therefore group the first six paragraphs (1:1 through 2:10) together and entitle this combination of paragraphs: "Jonah's First Commission." Obviously, the remaining paragraphs beginning with 3:1 to the close of the book can be combined under the title: "Jonah's Second Commission." We place these two titles with the numbers of the chapters which they cover under the appropriate diagonal lines in the chart. (See Figure 3.)

We now have an even clearer picture of the entire book and can easily think through its contents because its structure is so plain.

In connection with Step 3, we need now to add the following instructions:

Addition to Step 3—"Titling"

The title of each main division should be general enough to cover the material and yet specific enough to focus in on the contents of that particular section.

Apply the "specific title" instruction to the chart on Jonah. Instead of titles like "Commission" and "Recommission" which would be too general for the two main divisions in the book of Jonah, we have used the more specific phrases "Jonah's First Commission" and "Jonah's Second Commission." It should be evident even to a casual reader of the Scriptures that the books of the Bible are not all structured alike and the outline of some books may not be as easy to identify as the outline of Jonah. In fact, it may often demand careful observation and examination before we are able to see how the parts of a book go together to make up the whole.

What are some other clues about a book's structure when an outline

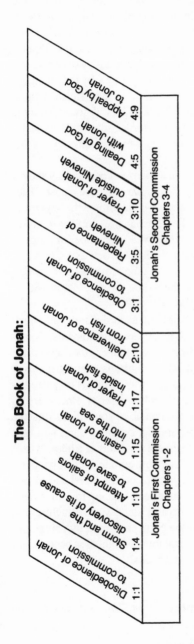

The Book of Jonah:

1:1 Disobedience of Jonah to commission

1:4 Storm and the discovery of its cause

1:10 Attempt of sailors to save Jonah

1:15 Casting of Jonah into the sea

1:17 Prayer of Jonah inside fish

2:10 Deliverance of Jonah from fish

Jonah's First Commission Chapters 1-2

3:1 Obedience of Jonah to commission

3:5 Repentance of Nineveh

3:10 Prayer of Jonah outside Nineveh

4:5 Dealing of God with Jonah

4:9 Appeal by God to Jonah

Jonah's Second Commission Chapters 3-4

Figure 3

is not readily apparent? Sometimes you will be able to discern the structure by the author's repetition of a significant word, phrase, or idea. A classic example of this is in 1 Corinthians (NASB) where the Apostle Paul uses the expression "now concerning" in 7:1; 7:25; 8:1, 4; 12:1; 16:1; and 16:12. Likewise the teaching ministry of Jesus is set forth in five different parts of the Gospel of Matthew by the repetition of the formula (or its equivalent) "when Jesus had finished these words" in chapter 7:28, 11:1, 13:53, 19:1, and 26:1. Another example is in 1 Peter 2:13 through 3:7 where the words "submit," "subject," and "likewise" are used to indicate the breaks in the framework of this section.

At other times a change of subject or a change of person may show a shift in the structure of a passage. For example, after the Apostle Paul deals with doctrinal matters in Ephesians 1-3, he turns at the beginning of chapter 4 to the practical side of the Christian life. Until we come to the close of chapter 5, he uses the word "walk" a number of times to refer to the way an individual should conduct himself as a Christian. Then from 5:22 through 6:9, Paul indicates the movement of thought from one paragraph to the next by the words "wives," "husbands," "children," "fathers," "masters," and "slaves."

We should also note that the number of main divisions in a book does not depend upon its length but rather upon its contents. Sometimes a comparatively brief book may have as many as five or six main parts while another book of considerable length may have just two or three. The difference will depend upon the way a book is organized or the method by which the author develops his material. But where no clues like those we have mentioned are available, you will find that the summary of the paragraphs or chapters in a synthetic chart will help immeasurably in the discovery of the main divisions of a book. These summaries will often enable you to see how certain successive paragraphs or chapters possess similar content or are so related to one another that they may be combined under one heading to form a main division. Ideally, one of the best ways to identify the structure of a lengthy book is also to summarize the book paragraph by paragraph, but this would obviously be impractical for we might then need a chart with sixty, seventy, or even more paragraphs!

Step 4—Looking for Subdivisions
Clarify the contents of each main division. This is done either by

further divisions into subdivisions with appropriate titles or by de-
scribing the contents of each main division from another perspective.
Place these clarifying titles under the main divisions on the chart and
directly in line with the paragraph groupings (indicated by the
diagonal lines) they represent.

The object of making subdivisions is to enable you to see the contents of each main division with greater clarity. In doing this, we need
to remember that everything in the chart should be stated concisely,
clearly, and accurately. So under the first main division in our chart of
Jonah we show the following subdivisions: Disobedience, Chastisement, Prayer; under the second main division: Obedience, Blessing,
Prayer. (See Figure 4.)

If we had treated the clarification of the two main divisions of Jonah
by describing them from another perspective instead of subdividing
them, we would have written under the first main division: Jonah's
disobedience and its remarkable sequence; under the second main division: Jonah's obedience and its remarkable sequence.

The Heartbeat of Jonah

One of the advantages of making a synthetic chart is that in the process of summarizing each paragraph we are compelled to read the text
attentively. In so doing, we are certain to make many observations
which would otherwise escape our notice. Let us note some significant
facts in this book.

When the Lord commissioned Jonah to go to Nineveh, He was actually calling the prophet to be His ambassador with a divine message
to a foreign nation. Jonah was the first foreign missionary in the Old
Testament, the first man ever called by God to proclaim a message to a
foreign country. Nevertheless, Jonah disobeyed.

Instead of obeying God's instructions, he boarded a ship bound for
Tarshish, fleeing, as he thought, from the presence of God. A terrible
storm broke upon the sea and the sailors became so afraid that all
called upon their false gods. Yet the one and only man on that boat
who knew the living and true God, the only individual who really
knew how to pray, was fast asleep, completely insensible to the need
of every one around him. Jonah had to be awakened by the captain of
the ship and begged to pray to his God. But even though a heathen man
pled with him in that hour of extremity to cry to God, we do not read

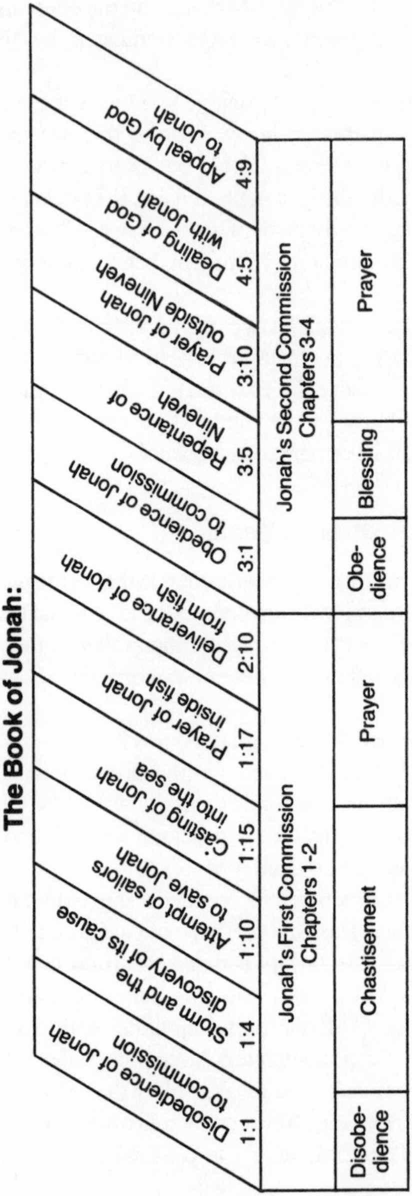

The Book of Jonah:

	1:1	1:4	1:10	1:15	1:17	2:10	3:1	3:5	3:10	4:5	4:9
	Disobedience of Jonah to commission	Storm and the discovery of its cause	Attempt of sailors to save Jonah	Casting of Jonah into the sea	Prayer of Jonah inside fish	Deliverance of Jonah from fish	Obedience of Jonah to commission	Repentance of Nineveh	Prayer of Jonah outside Nineveh	Dealing of God with Jonah	Appeal by God to Jonah
	Jonah's First Commission Chapters 1-2						Jonah's Second Commission Chapters 3-4				
	Disobedience	Chastisement			Prayer		Obedience	Blessing	Prayer		

Figure 4

that Jonah ever responded. Can you see any practical application from this?

We are also told that Jonah informed the sailors that if they would cast him into the sea the sea would become calm. How did Jonah know this? Remember, Jonah was the Lord's prophet. Although he might, for all intents and purposes, have wanted to resign his office as prophet when he got aboard the ship to Tarshish, the Lord kept him as His servant. Perhaps not fully realizing it at the time, Jonah was speaking prophetically that the sea would become calm should they throw him into the water. Nevertheless, the men did all they could to save his life. Only after all their attempts to row to land had failed did they cast Jonah into the sea. How sad it is that sometimes unbelievers show more kindness and concern for others than we, the Lord's people, do.

Skipping for the present the content of chapter 2, we then read of Jonah's ministry to Nineveh and the effect upon the king and the people. An entire city turned to the Lord! If, as we read in 4:11, there were 120,000 persons in Nineveh who did not know the difference between their right hand and their left (presumably infants), then the population of children, young people, and adults must have reached at least 600,000. No wonder that we read the expression, "Nineveh the great city" more than once in this book. What an unprecedented event this was when an entire city gave up its wicked ways to get right with God. What would we think if a large city in our own country turned completely to God in a matter of days?

We would expect the repentance of Nineveh to have caused Jonah to rejoice with all his heart because of the marvelous work the Lord accomplished through his ministry. How surprising to find instead that Jonah prayed, "LORD, is this not what I said when I was still at home? That is why I was so quick to flee to Tarshish. I knew that you are a gracious and compassionate God, slow to anger and abounding in love, a God who relents from sending calamity. Now, O LORD, take away my life, for it is better for me to die than to live." Instead of rejoicing in a great movement of the Spirit of God and the sparing of the city from destruction, Jonah became angry. It is obvious that his own heart was not right with God, but notice how tenderly the Lord dealt with His rebellious servant.

God points out to Jonah that he had more concern for his own personal comfort and interests than he had for a vast city in desperate need of being saved from certain and terrible destruction if they did not soon turn to God.

What a great and pointed message for us.

EXERCISE 1

In order to apply the techniques presented in this chapter, take time to construct a synthetic chart on 1 Thessalonians. If you follow the steps outlined in the preceding pages, you should not have much difficulty in doing this work. Do not read any book or commentary on the epistle. Create your own study tool! You *can* do it with the help of our wonder-working God, and you will be amazed at how much you will learn. Here are suggestions for paragraph divisions to help you get started: 1:1, 1:2-10, 2:1-12, 2:13-16, 2:17-20, 3:1-10, 3:11-13, 4:1-8, 4:9-12, 4:13-18, 5:1-11, 5:12-22, 5:23-24, 5:25, 5:26-27, 5:28.

When you finish with your study, turn to page 135 for a synthetic chart and discussion of 1 Thessalonians in Exercise 1.

2. THE SYNTHETIC APPROACH:

Discovering the Main Emphases

In our previous chapter, we learned the basic procedure for constructing a synthetic chart of a book in the Bible. In the process, we found that this approach to Bible study can be of significant help in gaining an understanding and appreciation of the overall structure of a book and how the individual parts of that book fit together to form the whole.

But our job of synthesis is not yet complete. As we will discover in this chapter, our synthetic chart can be enhanced by adding to it prominent features or items of special emphasis from the book we are studying.

The discovery of these will enable us to gain a much better perspective of a book and may suggest the reason or reasons the book was written, as well as the message the book has for us today.

Discovering the Main Emphases in a Book

There are at least two ways to determine the important emphases or distinctives in a book. We will explore them by noting their use in the books of Exodus, Luke, and Hebrews.

Repeated Words or Ideas

First, we should observe if a significant word, phrase, idea, or concept is repeated in a book and how that key word or concept is used to develop the structure or theme of the book.

For example, the word "better" is used repeatedly throughout the book of Hebrews. This is because one of the main goals of the writer is to prove Christ's superiority over angels, over prophets, over Moses, over Joshua, and over the Aaronic and Levitical priesthoods. Therefore, the book contains several prominent distinctives. It contains a contrast between the Old Covenant and the New Covenant, showing that the New Covenant is better than the Old. It contains a contrast between the Old Testament sacrifices and Christ's sacrifice to show the superiority of Christ's sacrifice. It shows the contrast between the Canaan rest and the believer's better rest in Christ. It reveals the contrast between the Aaronic priesthood and the Melchizedekan priesthood so that we may see how the latter, being typical of the priesthood of the Lord Jesus Christ, is far better than the former.

Another example with a number of interesting distinctives is the Gospel of Luke. In this Gospel, the title "Son of Man" is used more frequently than in any of the other three Gospels. As we read through the book, we discern that the writer, without detracting from Christ's deity, draws our attention over and over again to His humanity.

There are more details in Luke about the birth of Jesus than in any other Gospel. Yet the writer is careful to state that Christ's birth was miraculous and would show that He is divine. Furthermore, Luke tells of the boyhood of Christ while revealing His uniqueness when he describes how the doctors of the law were "asking Him questions." Also there are numerous references to Christ's eating of food, all of which demonstrate the reality of His manhood (7:36, 11:37, 14:1, 24:30, and 24:42-43).

Again, Luke describes Christ's frequent praying. He prays at His baptism (3:21), after performing miracles (5:16), before appointing the twelve apostles (6:12), just before His transfiguration (9:28, 29), for His murderers (23:34), and also with His last breath on the cross (23:46). As a man, Jesus was dependent upon His Father and there is more about His prayer life in this Gospel than in any of the other three. Toward the end of his Gospel, Luke includes the statements of two individuals who declared Christ's manhood: the repentant thief on the cross—"This man has done nothing wrong"—and the centurion—"Certainly this man was innocent" (23:41, 47 NASB).

One of the obvious purposes, then, of the writer of the third Gospel was to reveal Christ in His humanity. Luke also refers constantly to matters of human interest. For instance, he gives prominence to the poor and the outcast, and shows how the Lord Jesus receives them and loves them. Women are also given a more prominent place than in any other Gospel, with a number of them mentioned by name. Time and again this Gospel speaks of the common interests and concerns of humanity, as well as the relationship of Christ to men, women, and children in the daily affairs of life.

A third distinctive in the Gospel of Luke is the inclusion of the holy songs. These include the "Ave Maria" or song of the annunciation (1:28-33), the "Magnificat" or song of the Virgin Mary (1:46-55), the "Benedictus" or song of Zacharias (1:68-79), the "Gloria in Excelsis" or song of the angels (2:14), and the "Nunc Dimittis" or song of Simeon (2:29-32). All of these are connected with the birth of Christ.

These examples from Hebrews and Luke should be sufficient to show how the repetition of significant words, phrases, ideas, or concepts may indicate a book's prominent features and give a clue as to why the book was written.

Space Devoted to Particular Subjects

A *second* way to determine the important emphases or distinctives in a book is to observe the amount of space devoted to a particular subject.

In Luke we find that a large proportion of the book describes Christ's passion and resurrection. In fact, although this Gospel covers fifty pages in an ordinary Bible, seven pages are used to describe these events. The reason for this should be clear, for the perfect life of the Son of Man could not have been lived for our salvation without His suffering, death, and resurrection. For this same reason, large sections of the other three Gospels are devoted to a description of Christ's last days on earth.

Another striking example of how the Holy Spirit employs considerable space in order to emphasize a concept is found in Exodus. In this book of forty chapters, the first eighteen describe the conditions of God's people in Egypt and their deliverance from bondage. The next six chapters (19-24) discuss the law. The remaining sixteen chapters (25-40) deal mostly with the tabernacle, containing minute details about its construction and relationship to the priesthood. One of the reasons for the volume of material about the tabernacle must surely be to impress us with the importance to God of the worship of His people. He was not satisfied merely to save them from bondage and to give them laws by which they were to live in accordance with His holiness. He desired their fellowship, a fellowship which could only be established and maintained on the basis of blood sacrifice.

By summarizing the contents of a book's paragraphs or chapters in a synthetic chart, we can readily calculate the space devoted to a subject or concept and learn what may be one of the purposes for the writing of the book.

In Chapter 1 we presented four steps in the construction of a synthetic chart of a book. We are now ready to consider two more steps in the expansion of the synthetic chart.

Step 5—Charting the Main Emphases

Carefully consider the contents of the book and note in the chart the main emphases or distinctives of the book.

Classify or group together these main features using only brief words or phrases to describe each of them. Keep each group of ideas in parallel structure; properly match or balance them with each other in word number, word order, and word selection.

The Main Emphases in the Book of Jonah

As we look once more at Jonah, let us try to discover the items of special significance in its four brief chapters.

One of the arresting concepts in the book of Jonah is prayer. In chapter 1 we read that the sailors prayed when the storm overwhelmed them; they called on Jonah to pray; they prayed before they threw Jonah overboard. Chapter 2 is basically Jonah's prayer inside the fish. Chapter 3 contains a decree of the king of Nineveh urging his people to "call on God earnestly." And chapter 4 opens with Jonah requesting God to take his life because God had refrained from destroying Nineveh, the city to which he had preached but had no pity. In a comparatively small book, a substantial amount of space is given to the subject of prayer. In fact, each chapter of the book has some specific reference to it.

The observant reader will also have noted another prominent concept in the book—the subject of miracles. The storm in chapter 1 both began and subsided miraculously. Another miracle was the fish which the Lord appointed to swallow Jonah. It was the right size, it came to the right place, and it opened its mouth at the right time—when the disobedient prophet was thrown overboard. The preservation of the prophet inside the fish and his deliverance onto dry land are further instances of the miraculous.

Don't forget the plant God provided for Jonah outside Nineveh or the worm which destroyed it. They, too, were miracles.

The extraordinary effects of Jonah's ministry—an entire city, at least 600,000 strong, turning without hesitation to God—also qualify for the miraculous category.

A third prominent concept in the book of Jonah is repentance. The necessity for repentance is clearly implied in the warning Jonah was charged to bring to Nineveh in chapter 1:1, 2. Jonah correctly interpreted God's warning for Nineveh as an opportunity for the city to repent (4:2). Finally, the account of Nineveh's repentance (chapter 3) as well as the Lord's closing explanation of why the city was spared (4:10-11) underscore the importance of repentance as a theme in this book.

But there are other distinctive features besides these first three.

The word LORD occurs no less than twenty-six times in this book of only forty-eight verses. It is apparent, then, that the Holy Spirit intends for us to see in this name another feature of special significance. As we follow His name through the contents of the book, we observe that the Lord is revealed in this book in three special ways. He is seen in His control of all events or His sovereignty, in His mercy, and in His righteousness. (It would be helpful at this point in your study to investigate the development of these themes.)

One more unique observation can be made in the book of Jonah. Unlike many of the other books of the Bible, it contains significant items of contrast. These are so obvious it is evident the Spirit of God has specifically set them there for our observation and instruction.

The first is the contrast between the disobedience of Jonah and the obedience of Jonah. His disobedience is clearly set forth with all its tragic consequences in chapters 1 and 2, while his obedience with its impressive results is indicated in chapters 3 and 4.

It is quite startling that Jonah never did repent. Yes, he did go to Nineveh after his experience at sea, but it is clear as we come to chapter 4 that Jonah's heart had not been broken. He had not turned to God in repentance for his disobedience.

Finally, we see a contrast between Jonah's first prayer in chapter 2 and his second prayer in the first part of chapter 4. What a difference between these two prayers.

These then are the distinctive features of the book of Jonah: prayer, miracles, and repentance; the Lord seen in His sovereignty, in His mercy, and in His righteousness; and contrasts between the disobedience of Jonah and the obedience of Jonah, between the unrepentance of Jonah and the repentance of the Gentiles, and between the first

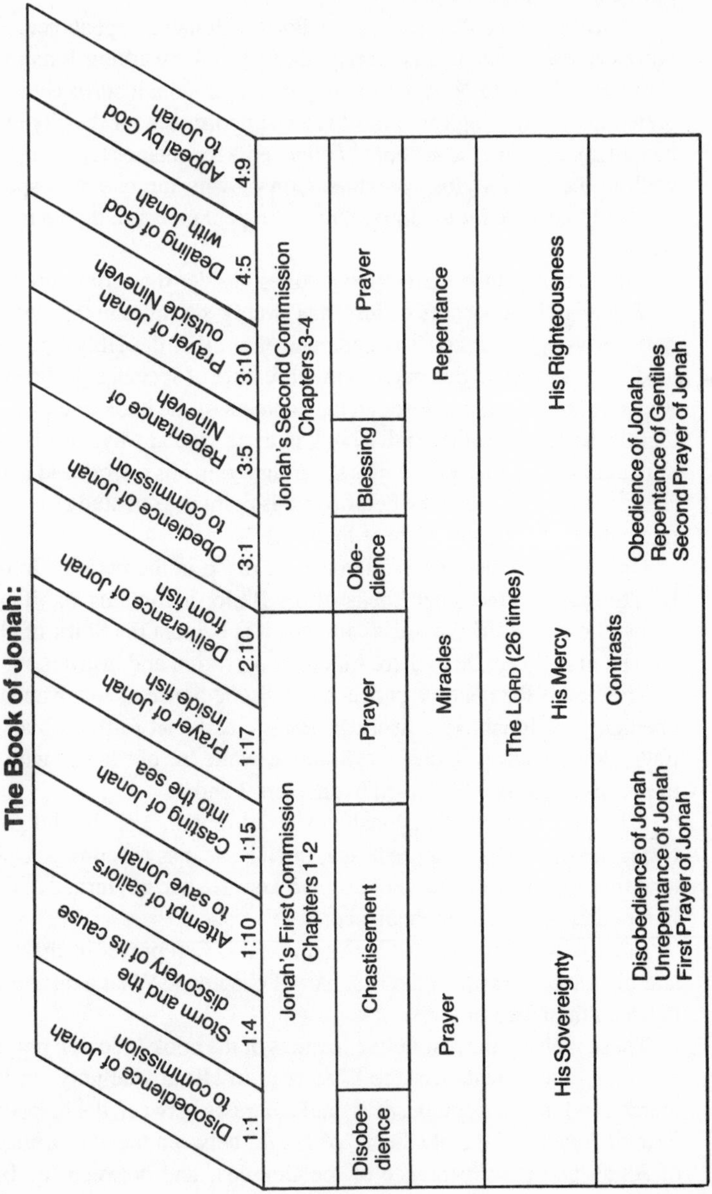

Figure 5

prayer of Jonah and the second prayer of Jonah.

Now that we have identified these distinctives, we need to record them on our synthetic chart. This is done by grouping them together beneath the previously added subdivisions. (See Figure 5.) Notice that all these important features are expressed in single words or phrases with each set of distinctives grouped together. These main features are now clearly seen as the distinctives of the book.

But the incorporation of all these concepts in a synthetic chart leaves us with a group of bare, cold facts. We need to ask ourselves what significance these emphases in the book of Jonah have for us today. This is where we need to depend on the teaching ministry of the Holy Spirit.

Surely one of the reasons the book of Jonah was written was to impress upon us that God is able to do exceeding abundantly beyond all that we can ask of Him, and He waits for us to believe Him and to trust Him to do great and mighty things for us. But as one of the other important concepts in the book of Jonah reminds us, and as other Scriptures affirm, this God of miracles does mighty things in answer to prayer.

We now add one final step for our construction of a synthetic chart.

Step 6

Summarize in a single phrase the contents of the entire book. This summary becomes the title of the book.

Write the title on the chart directly below the name of the book.

In the case of the book of Jonah our title is simply: "Jonah's Ministry to Nineveh." (See Figure 6.)

By observing the completed synthetic chart, we are now able to see the book as a whole and the relationship of the parts of the book to the whole. Because we have avoided cluttering the chart with extraneous details, we are also able to clearly observe the distinctives of the book. This is the goal of the synthetic approach.

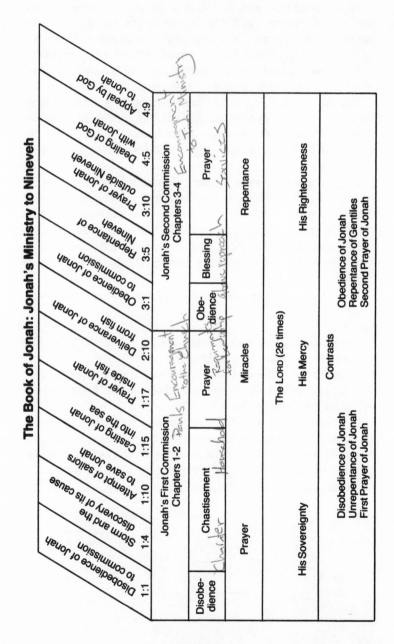

Figure 6

EXERCISE 2

Here is your next assignment. Without going to any outside helps, but by the examination of your own chart and mine on 1 Thessalonians, and by prayerful consideration of the text of the epistle, discuss if possible the main emphases of the book. Classify these concepts by grouping together those which are related to one another. Be sure to express your ideas briefly, without sacrificing clarity. Summarize the contents of 1 Thessalonians in a brief phrase and place it at the top as the title of your chart.

The second discussion of 1 Thessalonians along with a completed chart is included on page 138.

3. THE GEOGRAPHICAL APPROACH

Definition of Bible Geography

No one who wishes to know the Bible can expect to gain an adequate knowledge of its contents without a good acquaintance with the geography of Bible lands. This will include the names, locations, configurations, and elevations of countries, mountains, rivers, seas, and lakes; the climate and natural resources of a biblical region; and the distribution of the inhabitants of these areas including the location of the cities in which they dwelt.

The Fertile Crescent

The land mass of the Old Testament world embraces an area about one-third the size of the United States, excluding Alaska. More than half of this land consists of a vast, uninhabitable desert. Most of the people of the ancient world lived either in the region of the Nile River or in an area known as the "Fertile Crescent." This region consists of cultivable land extending west of the Jordan River and the Dead Sea, north through the land of Syria, eastward toward the Euphrates and Tigris rivers, and southeast through the broad Mesopotamian valley formed by these two rivers as they empty into the Persian Gulf.

The Fertile Crescent is rimmed on the west and north by tablelands which reach a height of 3,000 feet, and bordered in the northwest by high, impassable mountains. On its western edge is the Mediterranean Sea. Between the arms of this crescent lies the desert, stretching all the way to the Persian Gulf in the southeast to the Sinai and the Red Sea in the southwest.

Because of the topography of the area, the Fertile Crescent became the major land route for travel between regions to the east and north of

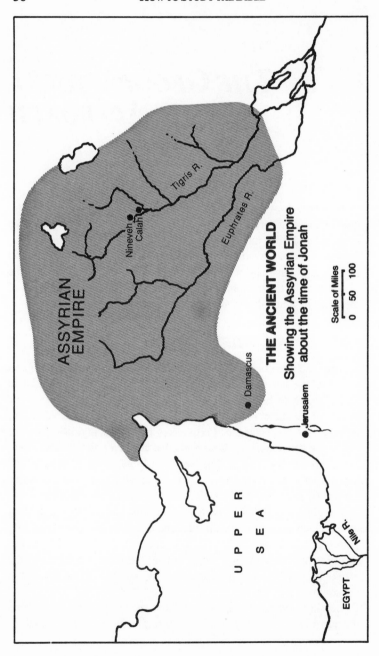

Figure 7

Palestine and the continent of Africa. Additionally, people who came by ship from the west went through the coastal area of Palestine to reach lands farther to the east. Thus, this region became the bridge through which all traffic between the west and southwest and the east and northeast converged. The land of Palestine became for many centuries one of the focal points of trade as well as of military conflict between Egypt, and the nations of Mesopotamia, and later Medo-Persia.

The Land of Palestine

Palestine itself is bounded on the east by a ridge of mountains over 3,000 feet in height, sloping steeply toward the eastern banks of the Jordan River. To the west, on the other side of the Jordan, another line of hills extends in a northerly direction from the Negeb, southwest of the Dead Sea, to a point a few miles southwest of the Sea of Galilee. A broken spur runs northwestward to the Mediterranean Sea to form Mount Carmel.

To the north, the hills of Lower Galilee, east of the Sea of Galilee, extend northward into Upper Galilee. Here they rise abruptly to over 3,000 feet and ascend further to the north in the Lebanon range to over 8,000 feet. To the east is the Anti-Lebanon range with snow-covered Mount Hermon rising to 9,232 feet. In the region to the south is a range of hills sloping toward the upper reaches of the Jordan River and the Sea of Galilee.

The entire region east of the Sea of Galilee, the Jordan, and the Dead Sea is a vast, mostly barren plateau, with some mountain areas in Gilead and Moab towering above 5,000 feet. The plateau extends further south into Edom where the mountains sometimes rise to 5,700 feet and are able to catch the remnants of moisture-laden clouds which pass over the lower country of the Negeb directly to the west. A coastal plain extends all the way from northern Palestine to the south, becoming wider as it goes further southward. It is broken by Mount Carmel which juts into the Mediterranean. The spur of the western highlands which runs northwestward and forms Mount Carmel encloses the plain of Esdraelon, bounded by the highlands of Lower Galilee to the north and Mount Gilboa to the west. This plain, sometimes called the Valley of Jezreel, provides the vital link between the coast and the Jordan valley and from there to Damascus and the eastern section of the Fertile Crescent.

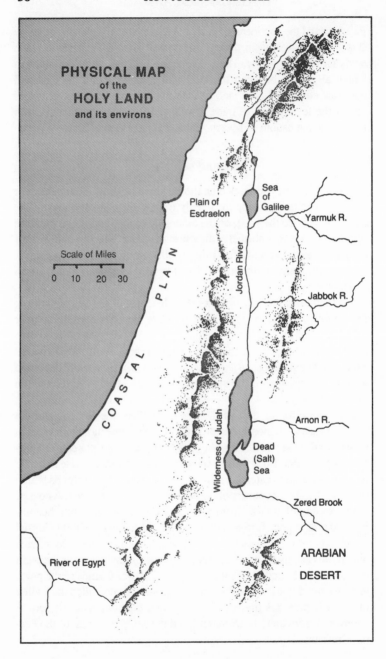

Figure 8

The principal river, the Jordan, originates in the melting snows of Mount Hermon, and flows southward to the Sea of Galilee some 650 feet below sea level. From there it continues to descend in a southerly direction until it empties into the Dead Sea, which is 1,284 feet below the Mediterranean. Thus, the entire Jordan valley is a vast trough which descends to the lowest land elevation on the earth. The rift continues southward beyond the Dead Sea, rising to a height of 650 feet above sea level before descending again and finally reaching the Red Sea.

With the exception of the Lebanon and Anti-Lebanon ranges in the extreme north, most of the mountains in and around Palestine are not high although they are often extremely difficult to traverse. In fact, in many areas the terrain is so rugged or precipitous that it is well nigh impossible to climb. Thus, travel in the Holy Land in Bible times was frequently an arduous and sometimes dangerous undertaking.

The Climate of Palestine

It has been well said that in Palestine the sea and the desert practically touch each other so that the climate of the entire region is greatly affected by these two opposing forces. Under these circumstances, the availability of fresh water is a matter of paramount importance.

The topography of the land effectively prevents all cool marine air from reaching the rift valley, creating an exceedingly dry and hot climate. On the other hand, the effect of the sea upon the western portion of the land creates a much wetter and milder climate there. The annual rainfall therefore varies greatly according to the topography of the land, with less than five inches in the Negeb and over forty inches in the mountains of Lebanon.

But while the coastal plains enjoy a mild and even temperature most of the year, sirocco winds blow in from the desert during two transitional periods: between winter and summer and again between summer and winter. These winds bring desert conditions to all of Palestine, including the coast by the Mediterranean, and last anywhere from a few days to a few weeks.

The peculiarity of the sirocco is that it not only causes the temperature to rise steeply but it also produces a drastic drop in humidity. The intense dryness of the atmosphere produces such great discomfort that people often become fretful and irritable toward others without any apparent provocation.

Jeremiah wrote about "a scorching wind from the barren heights in the desert blows toward my people" (Jeremiah 4:11), and Isaiah spoke of "his fierce blast [which] drives her out, as on a day the east wind blows" (Isaiah 27:8). No doubt it must have been a sirocco which brought so much misery to Jonah: "When the sun rose, God provided a scorching east wind, and the sun blazed on Jonah's head so that he grew faint. He wanted to die, and said, 'It would be better for me to die than to live' " (4:8).

The sirocco sometimes descends from the mountains to the coast with such force that it creates havoc for shipping, not only in the harbors along the shoreline but farther out to sea. How interesting, then, to read in Psalm 48:7: "You destroyed them like ships of Tarshish shattered by an east wind." It was while Jonah was on a boat bound for Tarshish that "the LORD sent a great wind on the sea, and such a violent storm arose that the ship threatened to break up" (1:4).

The Aid Which Geography Gives to a Study of the Book of Jonah

We have gone to some length to describe the geographical features of the lands of the ancient world and of Palestine in order that the reader may recognize the importance of this information for understanding even a brief portion of the Scriptures.

Now let us consider two or three other items in the book of Jonah to see even more clearly how the observation of geographical data is necessary to a proper comprehension of this book.

When the Lord commanded Jonah to go to Nineveh (1:1-2), He described it as "the great city," meaning, of course, that it was a city with a large population. By using this expression, the Lord sought to impress His servant with the solemnity of his obligation to carry out his mission. His work was to bear a message from God to a vast number of men, women, and children.

But where was Nineveh and where was Jonah at the time he received his commission to go to that city? By the use of a concordance or reference Bible, we discover that Jonah was a citizen of Gath-hepher (2 Kings 14:25). Presumably Jonah must have been somewhere in that vicinity when he received his call to go to Nineveh. Using a Bible atlas or the maps at the back of a Bible, we find that

Gath-hepher was in the northern part of Israel, three miles northeast of Nazareth and north of the plain of Esdraelon.

When we check the location of Nineveh on a map, we can calculate from the scale of miles that this city was some 570 miles northeast of Israel. Furthermore, as we have learned previously, a vast desert lay directly east of Israel making it necessary for a traveler from Israel to journey many extra miles toward the north before turning east toward Nineveh.

Thus our knowledge of Jonah's commission is enhanced by the fact that for Jonah to carry out the Lord's command he would have had to make a journey of tremendous length by the standards of those days. But Jonah's refusal to obey his divine Master was not due to any hardships or dangers which that long journey might have entailed, but was for an entirely different reason (4:2). It is not our purpose at this time to discuss the real reason for Jonah's disobedience, but through our study of geography we have come to a new appreciation of the dimensions of the task which the Lord gave to His servant.

Turning back to Jonah 1:3, we find that instead of going to Nineveh, "Jonah ran away from the LORD and headed for Tarshish. He went down to Joppa, where he found a ship bound for that port. After paying the fare, he went aboard and sailed for Tarshish to flee from the LORD."

Joppa is on the coast about sixty miles southwest of Gath-hepher, but Tarshish was much farther away. An inscription dating several centuries before Christ, which has been found on Sardinia in the middle of the Mediterranean, refers to a place called Tarshish that once existed on Sardinia. If this was where Jonah was headed, he was aiming to get to a place over 1,400 miles west of Joppa. But some geographers place Tarshish on the southeast coast of Spain near Gibraltar. If this was Jonah's destination, he would have to travel over 2,200 miles west from Joppa to get there. That was a long way to travel in those days, all in an attempt to get away from the Lord. Of course he could never have gotten away, and he found instead to his own discomfort that the Lord pursued him and overtook him wherever he went.

Instructions on Bible Geography

Some students never give time to the study of geographical data in the Bible. As a result, they have only a vague conception of important areas or places mentioned in the Scriptures and are unable to grasp the proper significance of those passages.

Here are some helpful suggestions for the study of Bible geography.

1. Note significant geographical references in the book of the Bible being studied.

Find out first what geographical data the biblical text provides before turning to reference works. It may seem much easier and quicker to go at once to a Bible dictionary or some other source of information to discover the material you need, but there is no substitute for observing the record in the inspired Scriptures.

Once we have seen what the Bible itself says, we may then use additional helps to gain further geographical information. For example, in order to discover where Jonah might have been when the Lord gave him the command to go to Nineveh, we use the reference in the margin of our Bible or a concordance. Those helps point us to 2 Kings 14:25 where we learn that Jonah came from Gath-hepher. Some Bibles have a condensed concordance in the back, but an unabridged concordance would be more helpful. A Bible dictionary or handbook will also give much valuable information.

2. Locate on a map the important places in the text.

Some chapters contain the names of numerous cities and towns, rivers and mountains, and other geographical features. If we are to get a proper perspective of a Bible passage, we need to see where the significant places are located. For instance, if we were studying the book of Joshua, we would find that chapters 13 through 22 describe the inheritance of the twelve tribes of Israel. Within these chapters are the names of several hundred cities with their suburbs. It would be an endless task to try to locate each city and town, but it is important to know the location of the territory of each tribe. Without reference to a map, it would be difficult to keep the territory of each tribe in mind and follow the book of Joshua.

Likewise, if our study is in one of the Gospels, it will be helpful for us to be acquainted with such significant areas as Judea, Galilee, Samaria, and Perea, as well as the Jordan River, the sea of Galilee, and some of the main cities and towns such as Jerusalem, Capernaum,

Bethany, Bethlehem, Bethsaida, and Cana.

Many Bibles have excellent maps at the back, together with an alphabetical index of most of the prominent places mentioned in the Bible. A good Bible dictionary or Bible encyclopedia will usually have helpful maps in the back covering the main periods of Bible history. Or you may wish to obtain one of the standard works on Bible geography mentioned in the suggested helps section at the back of this book.

3. Make note of the scale of miles on the map.

This will give you an idea of the distance between points. For example, by checking the scale of miles on a map of Palestine, we note that the distance between the southern tip of the Sea of Galilee and the northern tip of the Dead Sea is about sixty-five miles. Thus, when we read in Luke 2 about Mary traveling with Joseph from Nazareth in Galilee to Bethlehem in Judea before she gave birth to the Lord Jesus, we have an idea of the distance she had to travel.

4. Consult a relief map to acquaint yourself with the topography of the land.

As we have already learned, there is great variety in the terrain of Bible lands and a knowledge of the topography will often be of value in understanding various parts of the sacred text. For instance, when we realize that Jerusalem is situated on the crest of a ridge at an elevation of 2,500 feet, it helps us to understand David's expression "the tribes go up" to Jerusalem (Psalm 122:4). Also, when we note that Jericho is in the rift valley about 825 feet below sea level, we can appreciate more fully Christ's story of the man who "was going down from Jerusalem to Jericho" (Luke 10).

5. Draw your own map to impress certain geographical details in your mind.

In making your own map, note the following suggestions:

a) Do not spend too much time on the drawing of a map. A rough map which contains the information you need will be adequate.

b) Make the map clear by not cluttering it with too many details. A simple map showing the particulars which the map is intended to exhibit is better than an elaborate one in which there are too many items.

c) Show the distinction between certain items on the map by applying any of the following techniques:

(1) Use colors.

(2) Make shaded areas with parallel lines (diagonal, vertical, horizontal).

(3) Supply a legend or key to explain the differences in colors or shaded areas.

d) Draw lines with ordinary black lead for boundaries, roads, or other routes of travel. Where it is necessary to make a distinction in the lines, make them of different colors or draw dotted, dotted and dashed, or heavy and light lines.

EXERCISE 3

Paul started out on his second missionary journey from Antioch in Syria. In the course of time he reached Philippi, his first stop in Europe. From there he went to Thessalonica. His epistles to the Thessalonians were written not long after he had left that city.

Using the principles you have learned from this chapter, do your own research on the geography of 1 Thessalonians. Note first the important places mentioned in the epistle. Then refer to Acts 15:36-18:11. This passage describes Paul's second missionary journey, during which he visited Thessalonica. After completing your own research, obtain any extra information you can from a Bible dictionary or other resource. Use this information to draw a rough map of Greece, showing the important places described in 1 Thessalonians and Acts which help you to better understand the epistle.

4. THE CULTURAL APPROACH

Meaning of Culture

Culture refers to the distinctive characteristics of a racial, religious, or social group. That is, what people do—the way they live, the way they think, the way they act.

The Bible abounds in features of cultural significance. But we are so far removed from the people who lived in Bible times that it is difficult for us to comprehend their ways or even their patterns of thought and belief. Nevertheless, if we are to understand the Bible properly, we need to learn what we can about the culture of the various racial, religious, and social groups included in the biblical record.

It is impossible for us to know all about the specific traits, beliefs, traditions, and other characteristics which constituted any one of these ancient civilizations. But the more we can learn about them, the better we will be able to understand the Scriptures which were originally written to them, for them, and about them. Our study of cultural backgrounds will enable us to gain an understanding of the people to whom a book was written. This may include the circumstances in which they lived and the unique problems they faced. Obviously, culture and history overlap and we cannot consider the former without in some way noting the latter.

Some of the factors included in the culture of a people are their nationality, government, religion, language, literature, customs, social life, aims and aspirations, physical environment, geographical location, and relationships with nations around them.

Cultural Patterns in the Book of Jonah

We return, now, to our study of the book of Jonah to demonstrate the cultural approach to Bible study. We recommend that you stop at this point and read through Jonah once again.

If you were alert in your reading, you may have observed some of the following cultural patterns in these brief chapters:

1. Mode of transportation on the sea: a ship of some size in which Jonah could go below deck and sleep (1:5); a ship propelled by sails and oars (1:13).

2. Commercial arrangements: travel between Palestine and Tarshish; the carrying of passengers by a payment or fare (1:3).

3. Beliefs held by the sailors: false gods (1:5); casting of lots as a means of securing desired information (1:7).

4. Religious acts on the part of the sailors: prayer to false gods (1:5) and later to the God of Israel (1:14); sacrificing to the Lord and making vows (1:16).

5. Depraved moral conditions in Nineveh (1:2; 3:8, 10).

6. Well developed civilization in Nineveh: people living in a vast metropolis (1:2; 3:2, 3; 4:11); raising of cattle (3:7; 4:11).

7. System of government in Nineveh: a king who sat on the throne, exercised sovereignty, and ruled by decree; a number of nobles under the king's direct authority (3:6, 7).

8. Religious acts by the people of Nineveh: repentance (3:5-9); prayer to the God of Israel (3:8).

9. Modes of expressing repentance: fasting, covering oneself with sackcloth and ashes, and turning away from evil (3:5-8).

We have omitted reference to Jonah's own beliefs as we shall discuss these at a later time.

Helps to the Understanding of Cultural Backgrounds in Bible Times

An understanding of the customs of the Jews in both the Old and New Testaments is not as formidable a task as it may at first seem. This is because many of the religious and social practices of the chosen people had their roots in the Mosaic code promulgated in the Pentateuch. Jewish manners and customs which at first seem so difficult to interpret are much more comprehensible in light of the Mosaic law.

An example of this is the vow Hannah made to the Lord when she prayed that He would give her a son. We read in 1 Samuel 1:11 that

Hannah "made a vow, saying, 'O LORD Almighty, if you will only look upon your servant's misery and remember me, and not forget your servant but give her a son, then I will give him to the LORD for all the days of his life, and no razor will ever be used on his head.' "

What did Hannah mean when she spoke about a razor never being used on his head and him being given to the Lord all the days of his life?

With the use of a good reference Bible we are directed from 1 Samuel 1:11 to Numbers 6:1-21 where we read about the law of the Nazirite. By comparing the two passages, we see that Hannah promised the Lord that if He would answer her prayer she would give her son back to Him under the provisions of the Nazirite vow.

Later in this passage we find a further example of the contribution of the Mosaic law to our understanding of Jewish culture. We read in 1 Samuel 1:24-25 that "after he [Samuel] was weaned, she [Hannah] took the boy with her, young as he was, along with a three-year-old bull, an ephah of flour and a skin of wine, and brought him to the house of the LORD at Shiloh. When they had slaughtered the bull, they brought the boy to Eli." Again, the reference in the margin of our Bible directs us to Numbers 15:8-10 where we read the divine instructions about the offering to be made by the person who had made a vow to the Lord: " 'When you prepare a young bull as a burnt offering or sacrifice, for a special vow or a fellowship offering to the LORD, bring with the bull a grain offering of three-tenths of an ephah of fine flour mixed with half a hin of oil. Also bring half a hin of wine as a drink offering. It will be an offering made by fire, an aroma pleasing to the LORD.' " Hannah was obedient to the Lord's instruction.

Besides the information on cultural backgrounds which we are able to obtain from the Scriptures themselves, we can get a great deal of help from secular or extra-biblical sources. These sources contain the results of the labors of archaeologists, linguists, historians, geographers, and a host of others. Their work has contributed immeasurably to our understanding of the culture of those who lived in Bible lands during the times which are recorded in the Scriptures. Bible handbooks, Bible dictionaries, and Bible encyclopedias contain a vast wealth of this information on the culture of these ancient people and with such material readily accessible to us, we are able to obtain remarkable insights into their traditions, beliefs, and customs.

The subject of hospitality is a good example of this. Our Bible dictionaries and encyclopedias reveal that in these lands where desert conditions were prevalent, the entertainment of a guest was regarded as a right of a traveler and, therefore, the duty of the host. In fact, the guest did not even thank his host for the favor because sooner or later the host might himself become dependent upon someone's hospitality.

This throws light on the narrative in Judges 19:14-21 about the Levite and his concubine who "went on, and the sun set as they neared Gibeah in Benjamin. There they stopped to spend the night. They went and sat in the city square, but no one took them into his home for the night."

The fact that the Levite and his concubine sat in the town square was an indication that they needed hospitality. The failure of the people of the town to provide them with shelter was a great breach of etiquette. For the host was not only obligated to provide shelter for the traveler, but he was expected to defend his guest for three days from any intruder while the traveler was under his roof. The sin of Gibeah lay both in its failure to give hospitality to the Levite and his concubine and also in not providing safety for them while they were there. Contrast this with the treatment Laban offered to Abraham's servant when he arrived in Nahor to seek a bride for Isaac (Genesis 24:31).

Procedure for the Study of Cultural Backgrounds in a Book in the Bible

1. Read through the book and note those items which have cultural significance.

In this connection, observe any customs or features which were apparently in vogue at the time. We have mentioned earlier in this chapter some factors which are included in the culture of a people and these should indicate some of the specific items you should look for in the book you are studying. If we were to try to learn all there is to know about every cultural pattern in a given book, it would be an unending task. We must therefore depend upon the Holy Spirit and common sense to direct us in the selection of the cultural features which are important enough to deserve our attention and research.

Also, if the book is extensive it would not be possible to gather all this information at one time since there may be a vast amount of material which relates to the culture of the people. In one of the Gospels, for instance, there may be references to the synagogue; the Passover and other feasts of the Jews; baptism; the sabbath; Jewish laws relating to childbirth, marriage, and divorce; the Sanhedrin, the Pharisees, the Sadducees, and the scribes. Besides all this, there may be references to the Samaritans, the Romans, and certain procedures of Roman rule. In such a case, it may be well to learn what you can about the synagogue, the Sanhedrin, the three main parties involved in the opposition to Christ, and one or two other important items. The many other cultural patterns would then be left for a future date when you can become more involved in a careful study of the book, passage by passage or paragraph by paragraph.

Looking again at the book of Jonah, there are at least one or two cultural patterns which we believe are worthy of special consideration. The first of these is the racial differences of the individuals in the book. In 1:8 the sailors asked Jonah, " 'Tell us. . . . What do you do? Where do you come from? What is your country? From what people are you?' " It's clear that they would not have asked such questions if they were of the same nationality as he.

The Phoenicians were the great seafaring people of that day. In fact, long before that time the Phoenicians had supplied David and Solomon with timber from Lebanon for the construction of the palace and temple in Jerusalem. Their ships traveled in various directions both in the Red Sea and in the Mediterranean. It is known that by about 1,000 B.C. they had a sea lane to Spain. We therefore suppose that these mariners with whom Jonah was traveling were Phoenician, speaking a different language than he spoke.

The Ninevites, on the other hand, were Assyrian. Again, their language was different from that of the Hebrews and the Phoenicians. How then could Jonah have communicated effectively with the sailors and with the people of Nineveh? Scholars have discovered clear affinities between all Semitic dialects. This means that Accadian (the language of the Assyrians and Babylonians), Arabic, Hebrew, and Phoenician probably all came from the same linguistic source. We also know that about 100 years after Jonah's time, Aramaic served as the *lingua franca* or common language among these nations. This trade language was in official use from Assyria to Judah. It is conceivable that such a means of communication already existed in the time of Jonah although we have no verification of that possibility. Perhaps this is a reasonable explanation for Jonah's ability to communicate with the mariners on the ship and then later with the people of Nineveh.

At any rate Jonah must have had good linguistic ability to have been able to understand the sailors. In fact, he spoke so clearly to them that they understood all he had to tell them about the God of Israel, to whom they eventually prayed and offered sacrifices.

And the success of Jonah's ministry in Nineveh indicates that he was able to convey God's message to the people of that city in such an understandable manner that they accepted it and turned to God.

The peculiar custom of wearing sackcloth as a sign of repentance also deserves attention. We are told that the people of Nineveh "from the greatest to the least, put on sackcloth," that the king "took off his royal robes, covered himself with sackcloth and sat down in the dust," and that the king decreed that both "man and beast be covered with sackcloth. Let everyone call urgently on God. Let them give up their evil ways and their violence."

This sackcloth was a cheap but durable material made from the dark hair of a camel or goat. Because of its dark and scratchy texture, it was deemed an aid to self-chastisement. Together with the tossing of ashes over oneself, the wearing of sackcloth became a fitting outward expression of grief or penitence.

A look at a concordance reveals several references to this use in the Scriptures. For instance, when Jeremiah urged Judah to repent he called on them to wear sackcloth (Jeremiah 6:26). When the remnant from the captivity in Babylon repented in the days of Nehemiah, they "gathered together, fasting and wearing sackcloth, and having dust on their heads" (Nehemiah 9:1). The Lord Jesus also told the citizens of Chorazin and Bethsaida that if the people of Tyre and Sidon had witnessed the miracles He had performed in their midst, "they would have repented long ago in sackcloth and ashes" (Matthew 11:21).

Other references to the wearing of sackcloth as an indication of grief or distress are found in Genesis 37:34; 2 Samuel 3:31; Isaiah 37:1 and 58:5; and Daniel 9:3. The use of sackcloth as a sign of penitence was not confined to Israel but was also employed in Moab (Isaiah 15:3), Ammon (Jeremiah 49:3), and Tyre (Ezekiel 27:31).

Bas-reliefs depict the kings of Assyria with magnificent attire seated on stately thrones. In contrast, we see in Jonah the king of Nineveh stooping from his high place of dignity, removing his royal robe, and assuming his place of humiliation with the lowliest of his subjects, clothed in sackcloth and repenting in ashes. Thus, by every possible means the king as well as the people of Nineveh wanted to indicate the genuineness of their repentance both by outward expression and by inward penitence.

2. If possible, discover when the book was written.

In some cases we can get a general idea when a book was written by statements in the book itself. For example, the book of Hosea states specifically that, "the word of the LORD . . . came to Hosea son of Beeri during the reigns of Uzziah, Jotham, Ahaz and Hezekiah, kings of Judah, and during the reign of Jeroboam son of Joash king of Israel" (Hosea 1:1). A number of the Old Testament prophetic books are similarly dated.

Other statements in a book may give us a clue as to when it was written. References to Onesimus and Archippus in both the epistles to Philemon and to the Colossians suggest that these two epistles were probably penned at about the same time.

We have already seen that Jonah lived about the time of King Jeroboam II, who ascended the throne of Israel in the early part of the eighth century B.C. and reigned for forty years. Hence, the book of Jonah was probably written about this time.

3. Note the location of the people to whom the book was written.

This is often indicated by specific statements in the book. For example, Paul's epistles to the churches are addressed to Christians in specific locales. Peter's first epistle is written "to God's elect, strangers in the world, scattered throughout Pontus, Galatia, Cappadocia, Asia and Bithynia." In the event a book does not give any clue as to the location of the people for whom it was originally intended, the reader should then consult a good Bible dictionary, encyclopedia, handbook, or Old or New Testament introduction.

As for the book of Jonah, there is no statement within its four chapters to show for whom the book was originally intended. But the fact that Jonah was a prophet to the northern kingdom of Israel indicates that it was probably written to that audience.

4. Note facts of cultural significance about the people to whom the book was written.

Only by knowing important facts about the culture of a people will we be able to put ourselves in the shoes of those who were the first recipients of the divine message.

Take, for example, the book of Ruth. Unless we understand the custom of levirate marriage (Deuteronomy 25:5-10), we cannot get a proper perspective of the betrothal of Boaz to Ruth, which forms the main part of the narrative.

Likewise, we will not have a right appreciation of Paul's appeal on behalf of Onesimus, Philemon's runaway slave, unless we know about the practice of slavery in the Roman Empire during Paul's day.

As for the book of Jonah, we can learn from 1 and 2 Kings several facts of cultural significance about the people with whom Jonah lived. These people were the descendants of the ten tribes who revolted against Judah during the days of Rehoboam, son of Solomon, and formed the northern kingdom of Israel. Their first king, Jeroboam I, who came to the throne about 937 B.C., set up a new form of worship in Israel with the making of two golden calves, one in the extreme northern part of the kingdom and the other in the extreme southern part, to rival the worship of the living and true God in Jerusalem. This rival form of worship became the great sin of the northern kingdom.

God raised up prophets to call his people to repentance, but to no avail. The sin of Jeroboam I was perpetuated right down to the time of Jonah when Jeroboam II reigned as king of Israel. In addition to idolatry, corruption, immorality, and crime were rampant in the land. In the meantime, Assyria had become a great empire and was threatening to destroy Israel. Social conditions in Assyria rivaled those found in Israel. The very first verses of the book of Jonah speak about the wickedness of Nineveh, the capital of Assyria, and the king himself refers to the evil and violence in the hands of the populace (3:8). Archaeology reveals that drunkenness was a common practice among the Assyrians and sexual immorality was practiced flagrantly, even in public places. No wonder then that the Lord pronounced doom upon Nineveh and threatened to destroy it within forty days after Jonah's proclamation.

EXERCISE 4

We have already seen that 1 Thessalonians was written during Paul's second missionary journey while he was in Corinth. As the name of the epistle implies, it was written to the Christians living in Thessalonica. Do the following exercise on your own, making use of any outside helps necessary.

First, make a list of five cultural features found in 1 Thessalonians.

Second, note the different groups of individuals who originally composed the church at Thessalonica. (Hint: see Acts 17:1-11.)

Third, with the use of extra-biblical helps, note three or four other cultural features which throw light on the city of Thessalonica and the circumstances under which the people who composed the church in that city lived.

5. THE HISTORICAL APPROACH

The Bible is a historical book. In fact, many Old and New Testament books are called "historical books" because their contents are mainly a compilation of events. These are Joshua through Esther in the Old Testament, and the four Gospels and the Acts in the New. But many of the other books in the Bible are historical or contain historical portions.

The books of the Bible and indeed practically every passage in the Scriptures grows out of certain historical roots. When such books or passages are carefully considered and compared with other parts of Scripture, we find they are often vitally related to one another. It follows, therefore, that if we are to obtain a proper understanding of a book or passage, it is necessary to observe its historical background. This aspect of Bible study is all too often neglected and results in misconceptions and faulty interpretations of Scripture.

Meaning of the Study of Historical Backgrounds

The study of historical backgrounds is a method of biblical research by which we investigate vital events in a given book or passage or such events as are related to it to gain a better understanding of that portion of the Bible. Our investigation should include events in the area of politics, religion, sociology, and economics. Obviously a study of historical backgrounds embraces the culture of a people, for culture has to do not only with the distinctive characteristics of a racial, religious, or social group, but also with the general circumstances in which they lived and the unique problems they faced. In other words, culture is an integral part of history and in this way history and culture overlap.

Examples of the Use of Historical Backgrounds

Our first example of the importance of historical antecedents is from the book of Ruth. In the very first verse of the book we read: "In the days when the judges ruled, there was a famine in the land."

This initial statement refers us immediately to the preceding book of Judges. So if we are to obtain a proper view of the times in which the main characters in the book of Ruth lived, we need to know the conditions in the land of Israel as they are described in the book of Judges. As we read through Judges, particularly chapters 17 through 21, we learn that the country was in chaos with every man doing "as he saw fit."

Yet in the midst of these tragic circumstances, we see in the book of Ruth the sovereign hand of God moving silently and unobtrusively to fulfill His purposes for two godly individuals—Boaz and Ruth. Thus, the historical background of the book of Ruth impresses upon us that God is in ultimate control of all circumstances in the lives of His own and is abundantly able to fulfill His designs for them in spite of adverse conditions.

Our second example is Psalm 34. Read this psalm and note that the superscription indicates that it was written when David "feigned insanity before Abimelech, who drove him away, and he left."

Through the help of a concordance or reference Bible, we find the details of this incident in 1 Samuel 21:10-22:2. The earlier chapters in 1 Samuel relate how Saul hunted David and sought by every possible means to destroy him. Getting his eyes off the Lord and upon his circumstances, David fled from the land of Israel to seek refuge with Achish, king of Gath. (Apparently Abimelech [literally, "fatherly king"] was the Philistine title for king just as Caesar was used by the Romans or Czar by the Russians.) David could not have made a more foolish move than to have sought refuge with the very enemy of Israel instead of relying upon the Lord.

When the servants of Achish discovered David's identity, they immediately reported him to the king. When David heard this he was filled with consternation and tried to disguise himself by pretending to be insane. Psalm 34 reveals the terrible fear which came upon David at this time of imminent danger to his life (vv. 4, 6, 17, and 19). But David also discloses how desperately he prayed in his deep distress.

The Lord's answer to his cries of distress are detailed in 1 Samuel 21:14-22:1:

"Achish said to his servants, 'Look at the man! He is insane! Why bring him to me? Am I so short of madmen that you have to bring this fellow here to carry on like this in front of me? Must this man come into my house?' David left Gath and escaped to the cave of Adullam. When his brothers and his father's household heard about it, they went down to him there."

After David arrived in the cave, 400 men of Judah joined him there. It was on this occasion of deliverance that David wrote this song of exaltation and called on his companions in the cave to "glorify the LORD with me; let us exalt his name together" (Psalm 34:3). This psalm, then, reveals David's great joy and gratitude because of the deliverance of God, but it also shows us that David was not satisfied to praise the Lord himself, but taught his companions to rejoice with him.

The Historical Relationship of Some of the Books of the Bible to Other Portions of Scripture

There are many parts of the Bible based historically on other portions of Scripture. We will mention just a few.

The book of Judges can be understood only if we have first read the book of Joshua, while the book of Joshua has its roots in the Pentateuch. Also, most of the Old Testament prophetical books can be properly interpreted only when we read them in light of the historical events described in 1-2 Kings and 1-2 Chronicles. Similarly, the writings of the post-exilic prophets, Haggai, Zechariah, and Malachi, can be comprehended only as we connect them with the historical events recorded in Ezra and Nehemiah.

The same is true of Paul's church epistles in the New Testament. Their roots are embedded in the Old Testament, in the Gospels, and especially in the book of Acts. It is in Acts that we read of the conditions which existed at the time the epistles were penned or the events which took place when some of these churches were founded.

The Necessity of Extra-Biblical Sources in the Study of Historical Backgrounds

There are some books of Scripture for which we have no immediate or direct historical backgrounds in the Bible. Each of the four Gospels, for example, has no direct biblical source from which we can learn about the history of the times immediately preceding them. Between the writing of Malachi and the beginning of the New Testament era is a span of about four centuries, often called "the 400 silent years."

When the historical curtain fell upon the Old Testament scene, there was a Jewish remnant who had returned to Judah by permission of the kings of Persia. This return had occurred in the days of Ezra and Nehemiah in the sixth and fifth centuries B.C. At the same time, the vast majority of the Jews had chosen to remain in Babylon under the Persian rulers, where they lived not so much as captives but as colonists.

When we open the pages of the New Testament, we find God's people still in their land but now under the rule of Rome. The Samaritans are in occupation of a large portion of Palestine, virtually separating Judea in the south from Galilee in the north. Several important institutions are also in existence now which were either not in existence or were not mentioned in previous Scriptures. These include the Sanhedrin, the synagogue, and various religious and political groups.

What brought about the change between the conditions at the close of the Old Testament economy and the times of Christ? And what significance do these changes have in our understanding of the Gospels? How are we to learn about those 400 intervening years and the new political and social institutions which are recorded in the first four books of the New Testament?

Since there are no biblical passages to inform us about what took place during those silent years, we are obliged to depend upon extrabiblical sources to secure the information we need. In our study of historical backgrounds, then, we need to obtain our data not only from the Bible itself, but also from reliable secular sources. Fortunately, there are abundant materials available.

Excavation of archaeologists and the work of many scholars have contributed to our knowledge of the ancient civilizations of Egypt, Greece, Rome, and the Near East. Recent discoveries from caves and buried mounds in Bible lands, as well as the deciphering of cuneiform and hieroglyphic documents from extensive ancient libraries, are constantly enlarging our store of information about the history and culture of these people of antiquity. Much of this information has been conveniently compiled for us in up-to-date Bible handbooks, Bible dictionaries, and Bible encyclopedias, as well as in biblical archaeology works and in Old and New Testament introductions. With such volumes so accessible to us, it is possible for any student of the Bible to obtain a fair knowledge of historical backgrounds.

Procedure in the Study of Historical Backgrounds

Inasmuch as history includes to a large extent both geography and culture, part of our procedure for the study of historical backgrounds will be similar to the procedure we used in the two previous chapters. Nevertheless, it will be helpful to review these steps in order to gain a comprehensive picture of what is involved in the study of historical backgrounds.

We should also remember that in contrast to the study of culture, with its emphasis on customs, beliefs, and ways of thinking and acting, the study of history is concerned primarily with events.

When studying the historical background of a book, the following basic steps should be taken. However, we should avoid making our study too lengthy or exhaustive, but aim instead for just enough information to give a clear perspective of its background.

1. Read through the book repeatedly, noting any clues which may suggest reasons why the book was written.

It may be much easier and quicker to go directly to a reference book for the information we seek rather than to read the Bible itself. If we do so, we may indeed learn more about the Scriptures, but we will not learn more of the Bible itself. As we try to learn the purposes for the writing of the book, we need to discipline ourselves to go first to the Word of God to discover what it contains.

Here are some clues to be on the alert for:

a) A definite statement by the writer of his purpose for writing the book. A clear example of this is found in the Gospel of John, where the apostle states "these are written that you may believe that Jesus is the Christ, the Son of God, and that by believing you may have life in his name" (20:31).

b) Specific problems or needs mentioned by the author to those to whom he is writing. This was the case in Paul's first epistle to the Corinthians where the young church was beset with internal problems, schisms, contention, immorality, and pride over spiritual gifts.

c) Special emphases or distinctives in the book. As we have seen previously, every book in the Bible contains certain special emphases. These emphases are often indicated by the repetition of significant words, phrases, or concepts, or by the space given in the book to certain subjects.

In his first epistle, Peter refers again and again to suffering. Yet he also speaks of the living hope which believers have in the midst of their sufferings. Thus it becomes clear that at least one reason for the writing of 1 Peter was to acquaint the Christians who were about to suffer great persecution with the blessed hope which they had in the coming of Christ.

d) Significant events described in the book. When you study a book, even one which is not primarily of a historical nature, it may surprise you how much of it may refer to preceding events. Under such circumstances, it may be difficult to know which of these past events is of special significance.

Take, for example, the epistle of Paul to the Philippians. There are at least twelve items of a historical character in this brief book. When we reach the last half of chapter 4, we find Paul thanking the Christians at Philippi for their gifts to him—gifts given not just once, but over and over. And now with Paul a prisoner in Rome, the church at Philippi had sent Epaphroditus, one of their number, to deliver yet another gift to God's servant. It is clear, therefore, that at least one of the reasons Paul wrote this letter was to express his appreciation to the church at Philippi for their loving contributions to him. But Paul thanked not only them; he also had warm words of appreciation for Epaphroditus. As a faithful servant of the church, he had traveled almost 200 miles to reach Paul with the church's gifts and had risked his life for the apostle's sake.

With the help of a concordance or reference Bible, we find that the churches in Macedonia (that is, the churches at Philippi and Thessalonica) were the very poorest of the Christian assemblies (2 Corinthians 8:1-6). Yet Paul says concerning them, "out of the most severe trial, their overflowing joy and their extreme poverty welled up in rich generosity" (2 Corinthians 8:2). By noting this historical background, we also learn that the giving by the Christians at Philippi came not from people of means, but from those who were desperately poor. Their continual giving to Paul emphasizes how rich they were in liberality.

2. *Note pertinent information about the author*.

Be sure to look for any clues to the author's personality or biography in the book, as well as from other parts of the Bible. Complete your research in the Scriptures first; then consult extra-biblical sources for more information.

For instance, if we were studying the epistles of Peter we would need to know some important things about the writer. We can learn something about the life and character of Peter by reading his epistles, but if we want to discover some basic facts about this man it would be necessary for us to turn to the gospels and to the book of Acts. However, it is only by using an outside source that we can know how and when Peter met his death. One of the Bible encyclopedias quotes Eusebius, an early church historian, as saying that Peter was martyred by crucifixion during the persecutions that Nero carried out against the Christians in Rome in A.D. 64. Eusebius also reported Peter's request that he be crucified with his head downward.

With regard to the book of Jonah, Scripture does not mention who wrote it. It is generally assumed, however, that Jonah himself was the writer. Second Kings 14:23-27 informs us that Jonah was from Gath-Hepher, a little town a few miles southwest of the Sea of Galilee. Although he was indeed God's prophetic messenger, the book of Jonah makes it clear that he was a willful, ill-tempered man.

Because Jonah foretold the prosperity which would come to the Northern Kingdom of Israel under the reign of Jereboam II, king of Israel, who began his rule in the early part of the 8th century B.C., it is also assumed that he prophesied to the ten tribes of the Northern Kingdom.

3. *Learn where and when the book was written*.

Many books of the Bible give us definite information as to when and where they were written. Where this information is not specifically stated in the book, it is sometimes possible to uncover these facts by noting the historical backgrounds in other portions of Scripture. In the last chapter, for instance, we were able to peg when and where Paul wrote 1 Thessalonians by comparing that epistle with the historical record in the book of Acts. Just by discovering those pieces of information, we were able to gain a whole new perspective of the epistle.

After you have checked your biblical sources, then you may con-

sult a Bible introduction or some other reference book for additional
information if necessary.

*4. Make note of the significant facts about the intended recipients of
the book. Here there are two main areas to be considered.*

a) The culture of the people, including their nationality, language,
and location. As much as possible, investigate their general circumstances, keeping in mind their political, religious, social, and
economic status, as well as their philosophy of life, customs, and
thought patterns. Sometimes much of this information may be gleaned
from the book itself.

For example, by reading through Peter's first epistle we discern the
following facts about the individuals to whom he wrote. The recipients
of Peter's first epistle were Christians who had been dispersed as
aliens throughout Asia, in what is now known as Asia Minor. Although these believers had not seen Jesus Christ visibly, they
nevertheless believed in Him and loved Him. At least some of them
were servants or slaves, and to some degree they were all suffering for
their allegiance to the name of Christ.

Besides internal evidence from a particular book itself, we may
also glean cultural information from parallel historical sections of
Scripture. First Thessalonians, for instance, bears a vital connection
with the book of Acts. From the latter source we can gather significant
facts regarding the people who composed the early church which was
founded in Thessalonica.

b) Significant events in the history of the people. This should
cover such events as have bearing on our understanding of the book together with the conditions and times in which the book was written.
Since history and culture overlap, both important events and distinctive cultural features will necessarily have to be considered together.

Insofar as the people of Jonah's nation were concerned, they had
turned their backs on the Lord from the very beginning. Their first
king, Jeroboam I, who ruled over the ten tribes which broke away
from the house of David, ascended to the throne of the Northern Kingdom in about 937 B.C. In order to keep his people from going to
Jerusalem to worship in the temple, Jeroboam I immediately instituted
a rival religion in Israel by setting up two golden calves. From that
time on, the Northern Kingdom went into a steep spiritual decline,

with conditions growing from bad to worse as the years went by. In the meantime, however, God in His mercy raised up a succession of prophets to minister to the Northern Kingdom. These messengers were mighty preachers who pleaded with Israel to give up her idolatry and depravity and to return to the God of their fathers. Several of those divine spokesmen, notably Elijah and Elisha, accompanied their messages with miracles. First and 2 Kings report eight miracles performed by Elijah and sixteen by Elisha. But in connection with the ministries of both these men a most significant miracle took place: resurrection from the dead. During the ministry of Elijah, the son of a widow was raised to life. She lived in the city of Zarepheth, which was in the country of the Zidonians. During the ministry of Elisha, the second resurrection took place when God used Elisha to raise up the dead son of a Shunamite woman. This latter miracle of resurrection occurred within the boundaries of Israel itself. Then, after Elisha was dead, the Lord caused a third miracle of resurrection to take place and once again it occurred within the boundaries of Israel. This particular instance occurred when a group of people were burying a man in the same sepulchre where Elisha had been entombed. We read in 2 Kings 13 that "when the body touched Elisha's bones, the man came to life and stood up on his feet" (2 Kings 13:21).

Can we even begin to imagine how the news must have spread far and wide each time one of these miracles of resurrection took place? Surely these extraordinary signs should have stirred Israel to give heed to the messages of God's prophets and to turn back to Him before it was too late. But tragically, even these miracles of resurrection seemed to have no major effect on the spiritual life of the people.

5. *As a result of your research state the reasons or purposes for the writing of the book.*

Having completed your historical background research, draw some conclusions as to why the book was written. Then check your work with a biblical reference book and add any extra information that you may be able to acquire.

Let's try to discern the purpose the author had for writing Jonah. Matthew 12:39, 40 and Luke 11:29, 30 indicate that in some way which is not mentioned in the book itself, Jonah was a sign of resurrection to the people of Nineveh. Some think that as a result of being inside the fish, Jonah's skin became so strangely discolored that he had to explain to the people of Nineveh what had happened to him. Others think that one or two of the sailors from the ship on which the prophet sailed might have seen him. Recognizing the man whom they had cast into the sea, they realized that he had virtually risen from the dead and they spread the news far and wide. Whatever the explanation, Jonah, who had been entombed inside a fish for three days and nights, came into the city of Nineveh as one who had been raised from the dead.

We see a striking contrast between Nineveh's repentance and Israel's obduracy. Nineveh had been sent only one messenger from God, who had preached only one message. Furthermore, the city had been given only one sign from God and only one opportunity to respond—yet this heathen city repented. The Northern Kingdom of Israel, on the other hand, had had several messengers, many messages, numerous signs, and many opportunities—yet she had still remained unrepentant.

As a result of all our research on the background of the book of Jonah, we may conclude that there were two reasons the book was written.

1. To teach Israel that God loves Gentile and Jew alike and is concerned for the salvation of both.

2. To summon Israel once more to repentance. Israel had in the past disregarded all of the Lord's gracious pleadings through His prophets. The example of Nineveh's repentance was another call from God to Israel to return to Him.

EXERCISE 5

If you have done the previous assignments, you will find that you have actually prepared a good portion of this assignment. Prepare a brief paper on the historical background of 1 Thessalonians, covering the following points:

1. Pertinent information about the author
2. Time and place of writing
3. Significant facts about the recipients of the epistle
4. Purpose of the writing of the letter

Remember to use your Bible first in your research. Consult extra-biblical sources only when you have thoroughly examined the Scriptures.

6. THE BIOGRAPHICAL APPROACH

A great portion of the Bible is an inspired historical record. But as we read it, we find that this book is at the same time an inexhaustible treasure of biography. In it we come across individuals from every walk and circumstance of life. We read about kings and queens, citizens and slaves, artisans and farmers, soldiers and sailors, the rich and the poor, the old and the young, the educated and the uneducated, the refined and the unrefined, the saint and the sinner.

Unlike many biographies, which often conceal the worst and exhibit the best, the stories in Scripture describe people exactly as they were. On the one hand many of them exhibited true nobility and greatness. On the other hand, we read of individuals with flaws and imperfections of every kind. In some cases the very person who is upheld as a model of faith and virtue performs deeds that shock us—until we look at our own hearts and see that the same capabilities lie within us. So while the virtues of the saints are listed for our edification and encouragement, the evil deeds of sinful men and women are recorded for our warning, lest we succumb to the same temptations.

Since these are biographies of real men and real women, with the same wants and needs, the same goals and temptations, the same hopes and fears as we have today, their study can be both intensely interesting and practical. As we examine these lives we will see our own lives mirrored in some of them. We may also find that their problems are our problems, their temptations are our temptations, and the reasons for their successes or failures are essentially the same as our own.

Definition of Biblical Biography

What precisely do we mean by the term "biblical biography"? It is simply the history of an individual as recorded in the Bible. This will include all events relating to his life as well as any clues the text gives to his personality.

There are nearly 3,000 individuals mentioned in the Scriptures. In the course of a biographical study, we must observe two cautions.

First, we must be careful not to confuse certain individuals who bear the same name but are entirely different personalities. For example, in the New Testament we find five women named Mary, five men named James, and five named John. And in the entire Bible there are some twenty persons who go by the name of Nathan.

We must also make sure that we do not confuse individuals who appear in similar narratives. The incident described in Luke 7:36-40, in which a woman anointed the Lord's feet with expensive perfume, is very similar to the story of Mary of Bethany, told in Mark 14:3-9 and John 12:1-8. Yet the similarities in the stories do not mean that the woman described in Luke's account is Mary.

Sometimes one may find that the records of obscure individuals in the Bible contain a wealth of information which will repay diligent research. Take, for example, Shaphan, the son of Azaliah. His name occurs mainly in 2 Kings chapter 22 and 2 Chronicles chapter 34, with scattered references in 2 Kings 25, in seven different chapters in Jeremiah, and once in Ezekiel.

We find that these references not only mention Shaphan himself but also several of his relatives. His grandfather Meshullam is mentioned once, and his father, Azaliah, twice. His four sons are mentioned a number of times. Of these, Ahikam is referred to nineteen times by name, Gemariah four times, Elasah once, and Jaazaniah once. Two grandsons are also spoken of, Michaiah twice, and Gedaliah twenty-seven times.

The references to Shaphan's father and grandfather do not yield any significant information, but a careful examination of the other scriptures and their context is more fruitful.

From 2 Kings 22 and 2 Chronicles 34 we learn that Shaphan was secretary to Josiah, the godly king of Judah whose father Amon and grandfather Manasseh had led the nation into the greatest depths of depravity and idolatry. At the command of Josiah, Shaphan took an active part in repairing the temple of the Lord in Jerusalem. When Hilkiah, the high priest, discovered the Book of the Lord in the temple, Shaphan read it to the king. Together with other godly men,

Shaphan also had an important role in supporting the king in his efforts to bring about a spiritual reformation in the land.

Ahikam is mentioned in 2 Kings 22:12 and 2 Chronicles 34:20 as "the son of Shaphan." Together with his father and three others, Ahikam was ordered by Josiah to inquire of the Lord because of the guilt of Judah. After Josiah's death, when Jehoiakim the wicked king of Judah was on the throne, Jeremiah prophesied against Jerusalem and foretold her destruction. His prophecy incensed the king and the people to such a degree that he would have been killed, but "Ahikam son of Shaphan supported Jeremiah, and so he was not handed over to the people to be put to death" (Jeremiah 26:24).

Jeremiah 36:10-11 makes specific reference to "Gemariah son of Shaphan the secretary" as an individual who owned the house from which Baruch the scribe "read to all the people . . . the words of Jeremiah from the scroll." This same Gemariah, in conjunction with two others, later attempted unsuccessfully to prevent Jehoiakim, the evil king of Judah, from burning the scroll which Baruch had copied, containing the words of the prophet Jeremiah.

In Jeremiah 29:3 we read of "Elasah son of Shaphan" as one of the two men to whom Jeremiah entrusted a letter he wrote to the exiles of Judah carried away into Babylon by Nebuchadnezzar.

Then in Jeremiah 36:11 we read of one of Shaphan's grandsons, "Micaiah son of Gemariah, the son of Shaphan." The context reveals that this grandson was the man who reported to the elders, including his father Gemariah, all the words of the Lord spoken through Jeremiah which Baruch had read to the people from the scroll. Thus Micaiah appears to have actively supported Jeremiah in his ministry in the dark days of Judah's spiritual decline.

Also, in Jeremiah chapters 39, 40, and 41, we read repeatedly of "Gedaliah son of Ahikam, the son of Shaphan." The Babylonians appointed Gedaliah to govern the remnant of the people of Judah they left behind after carrying most of the inhabitants of the land into captivity. The Babylonians also turned Jeremiah over to the care of Gedaliah and he, in turn, seems to have supported the ministry of the Lord's prophet. However, Gedaliah was assassinated shortly afterwards.

Finally, in Ezekiel 8:11 we read of "Jaazaniah son of Shaphan" whom Ezekiel saw in a vision as one of seventy idolators standing in the temple in Jerusalem. Extra-biblical sources indicate that the name Jaazaniah was common in biblical times, but the attachment "son of

Shaphan" to this man's name indicates that he belonged to the same family as the one which we have been discussing.

We have gone to some length in following through the biography of Shaphan in the Scriptures to show that what appears at first sight to be insignificant and unimportant may lead us to some noteworthy discoveries. Here we find in Shaphan a godly man living in a momentous time in Judah's history, with three sons who provided spiritual leadership to the nation in an even darker era than when their father lived, and two grandsons who also supported the cause of righteousness and the work of God. Thus we see three successive generations of men who had a godly influence at a time when their influence was needed the most. Unfortunately, one son evidently went wrong. Were this a secular story, we would like to read that all of Shaphan's children turned out right, but the Word of God speaks truthfully. No doubt this boy lived under the same godly influence as his three brothers, but for reasons which the Bible does not relate, he went astray. Surely there are many more important truths we can glean from this biography of one little-known Old Testament saint, gathered from only a few scattered references.

Types of Biographical Study

There are five basic ways we may develop a biographical study.

Narrative Approach

In the narrative approach, we take up the history of the individual in the general order in which it occurs in the Bible. In an approach such as this, features of an individual's character will usually be mentioned during the development of the narrative. Take the life of Samson as an example. We can outline his biography chronologically, as described in Judges 13-16, as follows:

His godly parentage
His birth and early life
His contests with the Philistines
His involvement with a harlot and with Delilah
His captivity and his death

Most of the biographies in the Bible can be treated in this way.

The biographies of some individuals cover many chapters and even entire books in the Bible. The life story of Moses, for example, begins in Exodus 1 and continues through Deuteronomy. Even after that, there is reference to him again and again in the Scriptures, including the New Testament, where he appears with Jesus on the Mount of Transfiguration.

Another character whose biography covers an extended portion of the Scriptures is David. To read his story in its entirety involves examining 1 Samuel, all of 2 Samuel, the first chapter of 1 Kings, and a good portion of 1 Chronicles, not to mention the Psalms he wrote. Other references to him are scattered throughout Scripture.

There are many other individuals in the Bible with extensive biographies. Because the records of these people are so full, it is not possible to go into great detail in a biographical study. Instead, it may be best for us to satisfy ourselves with dealing with certain periods in the lives of these men, and with discovering the salient features of their characters.

Most biographies, however, are contained in a single book in the Bible. For instance, the story of Naaman is found in 2 Kings 5 with a brief reference also to him in Luke 4:27. We can sum up the first fifteen verses of this chapter by concentrating on the following main facts in connection with Naaman:

1. The description of Naaman
   a) He was a great man (v. 1)
   b) He was also a leprous man (v. 1)
2. The testimony to Naaman
   a) It was given just when he needed it (vv. 2-4)
   b) It was misunderstood by his master (vv. 5-7)
3. The cure for Naaman
   a) It was declared to him (vv. 8-10)
   b) It was rejected by him (vv. 11-12)
4. The healing of Naaman
   a) It was experienced by him (vv. 13-14)
   b) It was acknowledged by him (v. 15)

Since the Scriptures lend themselves to an infinite variety of treatment, we may take an entirely different approach to these same fifteen verses by discussing them from the point of view of the instruments which God used to bring Naaman to a knowledge of Himself.

> Leprosy, without which Naaman would never have sought the
> man of God (v. 1)
> The captive maiden from Israel (vv. 2-4)
> The heathen king of Syria (v. 5)
> The wicked king of Israel (vv. 6-7)
> Elisha, the man of God (vv. 8-9)
> The unnamed messenger who gave Elisha's message to Naaman
> (vv. 10-12)
> The servants of Naaman who had accepted the message given by
> Elisha's messenger (vv. 13-15)

Another approach is to list the various roles which an individual may have played during his life. For instance, we can look at David's life from the point of view of the following roles:

> As a shepherd
> As a fugitive
> As a king
> As a man of war
> As a broken penitent
> As the sweet singer of Israel

Or we may use the biography of Epaphras, which is recorded briefly in Colossians 1:6-8; 4:12, 13; and Philemon 23. Read these verses in the New Testament and then note the following characteristics of this Christian in the church at Colosse.

> He was a fellow believer.
> He was a beloved fellow worker.
> He was a faithful minister of Christ.
> He was an efficient Bible teacher.
> He was a great prayer warrior.
> He was a fellow prisoner with the apostle Paul.

We can learn a great deal from a careful consideration of the brief references to this New Testament saint.

Character Study.

In a character study, we are concerned with those traits which make up the individual's personality. Here again we may develop the study in the order in which the narrative is written, and set forth the elements of the individual's character as they are portrayed through the incidents described in the text. Or we may make a list of the individual's dominant qualities, the influences which developed these character traits, and the effects for good or bad which resulted. The order in which we list these character traits may depend upon the emphasis given to them in the narrative. Or we may prefer to note first the good features and then the bad, or vice versa.

Since the outstanding trait of Abraham is his faith, we may relate this quality to his biography (as recorded in Genesis 12-23) in this manner:

> His call to a life of faith (Genesis 12-13)
> The testings of his faith (Genesis 14-21)
> The perfecting of his faith (Genesis 22-23)

Combination of Narrative and Character Study

We may, at times, combine both narrative and character study in the same outline or treatise. Since you are now familiar with the biography of Naaman, consider the following biographical sketch in which we combine both the events of his life and his character:

1. The great but distressed man (v. 1). He was great in the eyes of the king and of the people of Syria, but distressed because of his leprosy.
2. The eager but haughty patient (vv. 2-12). He was eager to follow the advice of the little maid by going all the way to Israel to get healing, but was too haughty to accept the simple but divinely provided remedy.
3. The humble and grateful believer (vv. 13-15). He was humbled enough to go down into the muddy Jordan River, and grateful to be healed and to know the God of Israel.

Another way of combining narrative and character study in a biography is to follow the chronology of the subject's life with an evaluation of his character. In this way the events of a man's life become the setting in which we consider his character qualities. We might use this approach with the story of Jonah in the following way:

1. Jonah's background (2 Kings 15)
   a) His place of ministry
   b) His type of ministry
2. Jonah's ministry to Nineveh
   a) His first commission
   b) His second commission
3. Jonah's character
   a) His positive traits
   b) His negative traits

Linked Individuals

Certain persons in the Scriptures seem to be inseparably linked together as a result of some incident, and it hardly seems possible to consider one without also dealing with the other. Can we consider Boaz without dealing with Ruth? Or Delilah without Samson? Or Mary without Martha?

Note the striking contrast between Mary and Martha. Mary was occupied with Jesus in personal, unhurried, submissive, restful communion with Him. Martha, on the other hand, was occupied first in service for Jesus, restless, troubled, bitter, and self-centered, distracted by many things from Jesus.

Biography Made Relevant

Instead of making a list of events or character traits, this type of biography sees in the various incidents of an individual's life or in the traits of his character certain relevant applications to life today.

Take an incident in the life of Abraham for an example: In Genesis 18:22-23 and 19:27-29, we read of Abraham's intercession in behalf of Sodom. Taking these two portions of Scripture as the basis for our biographical study, we can learn three things which believers need to know about intercession:

The need for believers to intercede in behalf of others

The way in which believers should intercede for others

The wonderful results which may take place when believers intercede for others.

As another example, three times in the Bible (2 Chronicles 20:7,

Isaiah 41:8, James 2:23) Abraham is called the friend of God. We might study in Abraham those characteristics which make true fellowship with God real and possible.

Again, in the case of 2 Kings 5:1-4 we might use these brief verses about Naaman and the little maid to show how God sometimes uses unusual instruments to bring blessings to us.

1. God sometimes uses adversity or affliction to bring blessing to an individual (v. 1).
   a) The adversity may befall him at a time when he least anticipates or desires it.
   b) The adversity may appear to be a great tragedy.
2. God sometimes uses an insignificant individual as an instrument of blessing (vv. 2-4).
   a) This person may have gone through an experience of tragedy himself.
   b) This person has a right attitude.
   c) This person has a testimony to give.

Procedure in the Study of Biography in a Book in the Bible

1. Read the text.

Since our purpose is to make a study of a biblical character, the very first step we should take after we have chosen the individual who is to be the object of our research is to go directly to the Bible and read what it says about him.

As we have seen earlier, some biographies in the Bible are quite extensive. We therefore advise the beginner to start with a character whose history is contained for the most part in a single book. Gather all the information you can about the individual from that document. To get a fresh glimpse of this person, we suggest that you use a translation with which you are not familiar and read the book through at one sitting. Use a concordance to note all other references to the person in other parts of Scripture. If you are studying an Old Testament character, pay particular attention to any references to him in the New Testament. These references often have special significance in our understanding of the life and work of a person in the Old Testament.

2. Note all significant biographical facts.

Once you have read all the passages which deal with the subject you have chosen, read them again—and again! As you do, jot down any significant biographical facts you see. Be alert to observe items such as important events in the person's life, the responsibilities he was given, the opportunities he had, the problems or difficulties he faced, the responses he made, the successes or failures he experienced, the points of strength or of weakness in his character, the relationship he had with God and those around him, and the influences he had for good or for evil upon others.

Let us reread Jonah with an eye toward noting significant facts about his life. Since we have examined his life previously, we shall limit our study to his character traits.

Disobedience (1:1-3). The first thing we notice about Jonah is his willful disobedience. Having received a specific commission from the Lord to go to Nineveh with a solemn and important message, he deliberately refused to do it.

Pride (1:3). Jonah's pride went along with his disobedience. In proud defiance he insisted on going his own way rather than God's.

Insensitivity to human need (1:5, 6). The captain of the ship begged Jonah to pray to the Lord to save them from being drowned, but nothing in the text indicates that Jonah responded to that call in spite of the danger they were all in.

Honest confession of guilt (1:8-10). Jonah hid his guilt from the mariners. Only when they discovered that he was the cause of their peril did Jonah finally admit his wrongdoing. Unfortunately, he made his confession to men and not to God, and that only after he had been obliged to do so.

Obduracy (1:12-15). Jonah directed the punishment of his own iniquity when he told the sailors to throw him into the sea. But even as he spoke this, there was not a single expression of repentance on his part, even when it appeared that he would perish.

Faith (2:4, 8, 9). Jonah found himself inside the belly of the fish under the chastisement of the Lord, but he still showed no sign of repentance. In spite of his unrepentant state, however, we find him exercising an extraordinary faith. He spoke of the time when he would look again toward God's holy temple and pay his vows to the Lord.

Anger (4:1). Jonah was angry because God spared Nineveh. Jonah would rather have seen the city destroyed.

Faith once more (4:2). In his prayer, Jonah expresses his belief that, had he obeyed the Lord originally, God would have had mercy on the repentant Ninevites, according to His word.

Patriotism (4:2). Jonah's hatred of Nineveh stemmed from the fact that Nineveh was the enemy of Israel.

Petulance (4:3). Because Jonah could not have his own way he requested the Lord to take away his life.

Self-will (4:5). Instead of accepting God's way of dealing with Nineveh, Jonah in his arrogance demanded that the city be destroyed.

An unloving spirit (4:5). Jonah evinced no concern that the destruction of Nineveh meant the death of thousands of people.

Presumption (4:6-9). Knowing that the Lord in His holiness deals sternly with sin and wickedness (see chapter 1:1, 2; 3:4), yet Jonah dared to speak to the Lord in an insolent manner as though the Lord should condescend to Jonah.

Selfishness (4:10, 11). God, in His final comments to Jonah, showed the prophet that he was far more concerned about his own comforts and desires than about the lives of a vast number of people, including women and children.

3. Compare your research with other resources.

Outside resources such as Bible dictionaries, Bible encyclopedias, and other reference books may supply us with useful information about our subject which we may have missed. In addition, several excellent collections of biographies have appeared in recent years and are available in most Christian bookstores.

4. Organize your material.

You may organize the material you have gathered in various ways, depending on the amount of material you have collected and the objective you have in mind. A simple chronological arrangement is one method. Or you may wish to emphasize certain features of your subject's life. We have arranged Jonah's traits as follows:

Negative Traits	Positive Traits
disobedience (1:41-3)	honest confession of guilt (1:8-10)
pride (1:3)	faith (2:4, 8-9; 4:2)
insensitivity to human need (1:5, 6)	patriotism (4:2)
obduracy (1:12-15)	
anger (4:1)	
petulance (4:3)	
self-will (4:5)	
an unloving spirit (4:5)	
presumption (4:6-9)	
selfishness (4:10, 11)	

5. Apply the lessons.

One reason the Holy Spirit recorded so many stories of different people in the Bible was to give us examples to learn from. The record of these lives will reveal to us our own human nature. It will also show us mistakes to be avoided, the failures to which we are prone, and the successes we may achieve by the grace of God.

To apply the lessons which these biographies have to teach us, we must make a prayerful and careful evaluation of the facts we have gathered together. In many cases we will not be able to draw all the available applications from the biography of an individual, but we should certainly consider those which are of special importance or significance.

As we examine the character of Jonah, we cannot help observing that his faults seem to outweigh his admirable qualities. We may be puzzled at first when we think that a man of prayer and faith like Jonah could, at the same time, have been a person of such self-will and ill humor. But how many of us have to admit that a good proportion of Jonah's shortcomings are exactly the same as our own?

We may also see that Jonah persisted in his disobedience, for once having decided to go his own way rather than God's, he kept on with his willful way. Perhaps his response to God's second command to go to Nineveh was made, not out of a willing heart, but simply to avoid further chastisement. Jonah's conduct following his ministry to Nineveh shows that he remained unrepentant, wanting his own way to the very end. Thus, this study of Jonah's character teaches us that persistent willful sin in a believer's life may lead to such obstinacy that the heart becomes hardened. No wonder the Lord warns against becoming "hardened by sin's deceitfulness" (Hebrews 3:13).

Another important lesson we can learn is that when we become selfish and self-centered as Jonah became, then our own comforts and interests will assume greater importance to us than the salvation of men. Jonah showed more concern for the vine that sheltered him from the sun than he did for the salvation of the great city of Nineveh. The root cause of his peevish and ugly disposition was his unloving spirit. Had he only considered the example of the mariners, who tried everything they could to keep from throwing him overboard, his attitude might have been very different.

How very sad that this man who had such extraordinary faith was yet so lacking in love. Paul's words are appropriate here: "If I have the gift of prophecy and can fathom all mysteries and all knowledge, and if I have a faith that can move mountains, but have not love, I am nothing" (1 Corinthians 13:2).

Finally, because Jonah was out of touch with God, he misunderstood the purpose of the mission which God had entrusted to him. There existed a proud exclusivism among many of the Jews. Being the chosen race, they had the notion that salvation was not only of the Jews, but only for the Jews. In other words, no one had any hope of heaven unless he was a Jew or became a Jew.

Jonah seems to have had this very same attitude in spite of the fact that his two great predecessors, Elijah and Elisha, had ministered graciously to Gentiles. Perhaps this explains the reason for Jonah's refusal to obey the Lord at his first commission. As he indicated in his prayer (4:2), he was convinced that were he to preach to Nineveh as the Lord had commanded, the city would repent and the Lord would spare them from destruction. Jonah did not want the city to repent. Charged with patriotism, he hoped that the Lord would destroy Nineveh and thereby remove the terrible threat which Assyria was posing to Israel.

But Jonah made a terrible mistake. The real threat to Israel was not Assyria, but Israel's own unrepentance. Had Israel repented, as Nineveh did, the Lord would have spared the nation from the fearful destruction which awaited her.

As we look today at the desperate need of our own nation, this should bring a lesson home to our hearts. Are we occupied with trifles in this desperate hour as Jonah was? Are we concerned about our own interests and comforts and not about the condition of a world hurtling toward destruction? If this is the case, may the Lord bring us to the place of repentance, of utter brokenness and contriteness before Him.

EXERCISE 6

Prepare a character sketch on the apostle Paul, based on 1 Thessalonians. Support each trait you list with a Scripture reference. Note three of Paul's character traits which greatly influenced the Thessalonian believers. Prayerfully considering your list, check off those areas in which you fall short and suggest at least three practical steps you can take to improve.

7. THE SYNTHETIC APPROACH TO AN EXTENDED BOOK

The construction of a synthetic chart for an extended book in the Bible is essentially the same as that for a brief one. Since we shall be using the same principles we used in chapters 1 and 2, we will review these principles as we construct a chart of a longer book.

We have chosen for our synthetic study the book of Joshua, which has twenty-four chapters. In order that you may be able to follow our discussion effectively, please take the time to read through the book, preferably at one sitting.

Steps in the Construction of a Synthetic Chart for an Extended Book

Step 1—A Chart with Diagonal Lines
Place a sheet of paper horizontally before you. Draw a horizontal line across the center of the page. Then draw a series of diagonal lines leading out from the horizontal line at an angle of about 75 degrees.

Because Joshua 8:30-35 deals with an entirely different subject from all the previous verses in that chapter, we shall treat these six verses as a separate chapter and make a diagonal section for them. With twenty-four other chapters in the book besides 8:30-35, we thus require twenty-five diagonal spaces all together. Since we need so many diagonal spaces for this chart, we shall have to make each space considerably narrower than the ones we made in chapter 1 for the book of Jonah. See Figure 9.

Step 2—Summarizing the Chapters
Consider each successive chapter carefully and sum up its contents in a brief phrase of seven or eight words. Place your summary of each chapter in the corresponding diagonal space.

79

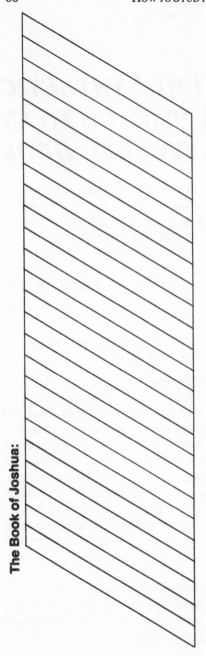

The Book of Joshua:

Figure 9

Joshua chapter 5 actually closes at verse 12. And chapter 6, concerning the taking of the city of Jericho, really begins with Joshua's vision of the captain of the hosts of the Lord described in 5:13-15. We shall therefore treat 5:1-12 as one section and 5:13-6:27 as the next section. Now, try to summarize each of the first five chapters yourself and write the results in the diagonal spaces provided in the chart. Remember that each summary should be properly balanced or mated with the others.

Having done chapters 1 through 5, continue with the rest of the chapters in the book. Don't forget that when you come to 8:30-35, you should treat this section as an individual chapter.

After you have completed the summary of each chapter of Joshua, compare your work with Figure 10.

Because Joshua has so many chapters, we have shown on our chart only the chapter number, not the verse which marks the beginning of each section. You will note that we have repeated the same title for the summary of chapter 4 as we did for chapter 3. At first sight chapter 4 seems to deal primarily with the memorial stones which Joshua commanded the representatives of each tribe to set up, but actually this chapter is a continuation of the story of the crossing of the Jordan. We could have made our chart more simple by grouping chapters 3 and 4 together under a single diagonal section.

Step 3—Selecting the Main Divisions

Group together successive related chapters to form the main divisions of the book. Indicate on the chart the chapters and verses which are included in each main division. Give each division an appropriate title.

Each division formed at this stage will represent one of the main divisions of the book. Some books, like Jonah, have just two main divisions, but others may have many more.

The title of each main division should be clear, but brief, and should be parallel in structure with the titles of the other divisions. The titles of the main divisions and the numbers of the chapters and verses may be indicated either above or below the diagonal sections on the chart. These titles with their chapter and verse divisions provide the basic outline of the book.

As you consider the summary of each of the initial chapters of Joshua, it should be clear that the first five chapters are separate from

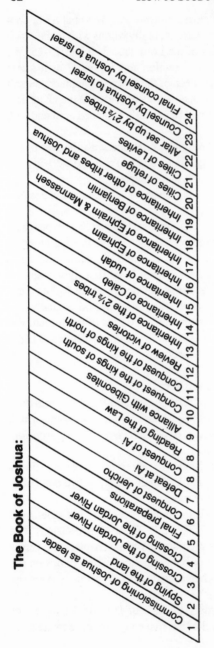

The Book of Joshua:

1. Commissioning of Joshua as leader
2. Spying of the land
3. Crossing of the Jordan River
4. Crossing of the Jordan River
5. Final preparations
6. Conquest of Jericho
7. Defeat at Ai
8. Conquest of Ai
8. Reading of the Law
9. Alliance with Gibeonites
10. Conquest of the kings of south
11. Conquest of the kings of north
12. Review of victories
13. Inheritance of the 2½ tribes
14. Inheritance of Caleb
15. Inheritance of Judah
16. Inheritance of Ephraim
17. Inheritance of Ephraim & Manasseh
18. Inheritance of Benjamin
19. Inheritance of other tribes and Joshua
20. Cities of refuge
21. Cities of Levites
22. Altar set up by 2½ tribes
23. Counsel by Joshua to Israel
24. Final counsel by Joshua to Israel

Figure 10

the others which follow. These should be regarded as the first main division. In light of the account which follows of Israel's possession of Canaan, how would you entitle this first section of the book?

By looking over the remaining chapter summaries, discover for yourself where the next natural break in the thought of the book takes place. This one should be easy to do. Give a title to this second group of chapters. Continue this process until you have completed your outline of the book. After you have done this, compare your outline with mine as shown in Figure 11.

Step 4—Summarizing the Content of the Main Divisions

Make a summary of the content of each main division. Place each summary directly under the main divisions on your chart.

When we made the chart on Jonah in chapter 1, we summarized the content of each of the main divisions by breaking up the main division into subdivisions. It is not always necessary to do it this way. Instead, sometimes we may summarize each main division simply by trying to see the portion of Scripture from a different perspective.

When you looked at Figure 11 a moment ago, you saw that our first main division was entitled Preparation for Conquest of the Land. We can summarize the contents of these same chapters with the words Victory Anticipated. Another summary might be Obstacles Overcome.

Try to complete the summary of each of the other main divisions yourself. Remember to keep this group of summaries in parallel structure, too. Now look at Figure 12 and compare your work with mine.

Step 5—Charting the Main Emphases

Discover the main emphases or distinctives in the book and place each set of distinctives at the bottom of the chart.

We learned in chapter 2 that there are two basic ways by which we may find the main features or distinctives in a book. First, note any significant words, phrases, or concepts which occur repeatedly. Second, consider the space given to a subject or concept in the book.

Can you recall any significant words or phrases which occur a number of times in Joshua? Turn to the first chapter of Joshua and read it over. There you will come across two important phrases which are repeated again and again in the chapter, and indeed, throughout most of the other twenty-three chapters of Joshua. Did you find those two

The Book of Joshua:

Chapter	Event	Section
1	Commissioning of Joshua as leader	Preparation for Conquest of the Land
2	Spying of the land	
3	Crossing of the Jordan River	
4	Crossing of the Jordan River	
5	Final preparations	
6	Conquest of Jericho	Conflict and Victory in the Land
7	Defeat at Ai	
8	Conquest of Ai	
8	Reading of the Law	
9	Alliance with Gibeonites	
10	Conquest of the kings of south	
11	Conquest of the kings of north	
12	Review of victories	
13	Inheritance of the 2½ tribes	Division and Appropriation of the Land
14	Inheritance of Caleb	
15	Inheritance of Judah	
16	Inheritance of Ephraim	
17	Inheritance of Ephraim	
18	Inheritance of Ephraim & Manasseh	
19	Inheritance of Benjamin	
20	Inheritance of other tribes and Joshua	
21	Cities of refuge	
22	Cities of Levites	
23	Altar set up by 2½ tribes	Counsel for Retention of the Land
24	Counsel by Joshua to Israel	
	Final counsel by Joshua to Israel	

Figure 11

The Book of Joshua:

	Preparation for Conquest of the Land	Conflict and Victory in the Land	Division and Appropriation of the Land	Counsel for Retention of the Land
1 Commissioning of Joshua as leader	Victory Anticipated			
2 Spying of the land	Victory Anticipated			
3 Crossing of the Jordan River	Victory Anticipated			
4 Crossing of the Jordan River	Victory Anticipated			
5 Final preparations	Victory Anticipated			
6 Conquest of Jericho		A Varied Success Achieved		
7 Defeat at Ai		A Varied Success Achieved		
8 Conquest of Ai		A Varied Success Achieved		
8 Reading of the Law		A Varied Success Achieved		
9 Alliance with Gibeonites		A Varied Success Achieved		
10 Conquest of the kings of south		A Varied Success Achieved		
11 Conquest of the kings of north		A Varied Success Achieved		
12 Review of victories		A Varied Success Achieved		
13 Inheritance of the 2½ tribes			Inheritance Possessed	
14 Inheritance of Caleb			Inheritance Possessed	
15 Inheritance of Judah			Inheritance Possessed	
16 Inheritance of Ephraim			Inheritance Possessed	
17 Inheritance of Ephraim & Manasseh			Inheritance Possessed	
18 Inheritance of Benjamin			Inheritance Possessed	
19 Inheritance of other tribes and Joshua			Inheritance Possessed	
20 Cities of refuge			Inheritance Possessed	
21 Cities of Levites			Inheritance Possessed	
22 Altar set up by 2½ tribes				Solemn Warnings Given
23 Counsel by Joshua to Israel				Solemn Warnings Given
24 Final counsel by Joshua to Israel				Solemn Warnings Given

Figure 12

phrases? They are "the LORD" and "the land." The first of these phrases occurs over a hundred times in the book. "The LORD" is thus one of the concepts which is given prominence in the book of Joshua.

At this point, take the time to read quickly through the book of Joshua. See for yourself in what ways "the LORD" is used in the book. Write your findings on a sheet of paper.

You will have observed such important statements as these which the Lord made to Joshua in chapter 1: " 'I will be with you; I will never leave you or forsake you' " (v. 5), " 'the LORD your God will be with you wherever you go' " (v. 9), " 'I am with you as I was with Moses' " (3:7), " 'the living God is among you' " (3:10), and "the LORD was with Joshua" (6:27). These quotations should be sufficient to indicate that the emphasis is on the presence of the Lord with Joshua and with Israel.

But another concept in relation to the Lord stands out just as forcibly as that of the Lord's presence. What do statements such as the following suggest to you in connection with the Lord? " 'No one will be able to stand up against you all the days of your life. As I was with Moses, so I will be with you' " (1:5); " 'We have heard how the LORD dried up the water of the Red Sea for you when you came out of Egypt, and what you did to Sihon and Og, the two kings of the Amorites east of the Jordan, whom you completely destroyed. When we heard of it, our hearts sank and everyone's courage failed because of you, for the LORD your God is God in heaven above and on the earth below' " (2:10-11). Read also 3:10-13, 17; 4:21-24; 6:2; and 8:1-2. Surely these references should be enough to enable us to see that here the emphasis is on the power of the Lord.

But there is another important concept relating to the Lord which we should be sure to see. Note the words of the Lord to Joshua: " 'I will never leave you or forsake you. Be strong and courageous, because you will lead these people to inherit the land I swore to their forefathers to give them' " (1:5-6). See also 1:15; 3:11-13 compared with chapter 3:14-17; 6:2 compared with 6:20, 21; 8:1, 2 compared with 8:24-29. There are other references of a similar kind in Joshua but these should be adequate to prove that the emphasis this time is on the faithfulness of God. In order to impress this thought indelibly upon the officers of Israel, the leader of God's people declared to them before his death, " 'Now I am about to go the way of all the earth. You know with all your heart and soul that not one of all the good promises the LORD your

God gave you has failed. Every promise has been fulfilled; not one has failed' " (23:14).

We now take these three concepts in relation to the Lord and place them at the bottom of our synthetic chart as we did with the first set of distinctives we found in Joshua.

The second significant phrase we found in the book of Joshua was "the land." Examine the diagonal section of our chart on Joshua and try to discover for yourself how "the land" is used. When you have finished your work, compare it with Figure 13.

How did we arrive at the various distinctives shown in Figure 13 other than those we have already mentioned? As we saw earlier, the phrase "the land" occurs numerous times throughout Joshua. In chapter 1, reference is made three times (vv. 2, 3, and 11) to the fact that this land was a gift by the Lord to His people Israel. This land, the gift of God to His people, became the place of blessing to Israel.

Now the book of Joshua emphasizes three special blessings which Israel received from God in the land. When you checked through the diagonal sections of your chart of Joshua, you could not have missed the fact that out of a book of twenty-four chapters, five chapters, most of which are of considerable length, are devoted almost exclusively to the subject of conquest or victory.

Ten chapters give detailed information about the inheritance of the twelve tribes. As you read the book of Joshua and came to the description of the inheritance of the tribes, you must have noticed how many places were mentioned in connection with their inheritance. In chapter 16, almost one hundred cities and towns are listed as the inheritance of the tribe of Judah alone. These ten chapters suggest the idea of the abundance or fullness which became the portion of God's people in the land.

The next concept is not as easy to discover because it is not as apparent as the others. However, if you will think through the contents of the book you will recall that reference is made several times to the rest which God gave to His people in the land of Canaan. In fact, the idea occurs several times throughout the book (1:15, 11:23, 14:15, 21:44). The idea is of such importance, that the writer of Hebrews mentions it in chapters 3 and 4 of his epistle.

But there were two underlying conditions which the people of Israel had to meet in order to experience these blessings which are set forth in Joshua. They had to believe God and they also had to obey

The Book of Joshua: The Occupation of the Land of Canaan by Joshua and the People of Israel

Chapter	Section				
1 Commissioning of Joshua as leader	Preparation for Conquest of the Land	Victory Anticipated	His Presence	Victory — By Faith	
2 Spying of the land					
3 Crossing of the Jordan River					
4 Crossing of the Jordan River					
5 Final preparations					
6 Conquest of Jericho	Conflict and Victory in the Land	A Varied Success Achieved			
7 Defeat at Ai					
8 Conquest of Ai					
9 Reading of the Law					
10 Alliance with Gibeonites					
11 Conquest of the kings of south			The LORD His Power	The Land Abundance	
12 Conquest of the kings of north					
13 Review of victories	Division and Appropriation of the Land	Inheritance Possessed			
14 Inheritance of the 2½ tribes					
15 Inheritance of Caleb					
16 Inheritance of Judah					
17 Inheritance of Ephraim					
18 Inheritance of Ephraim & Manasseh					
19 Inheritance of Benjamin					
20 Inheritance of other tribes and Joshua					
21 Cities of refuge					
22 Cities of Levites					
23 Altar set up by 2½ tribes	Counsel for Retention of the Land	Solemn Warnings Given	His Faithfulness	Rest — By Obedience	
24 Counsel by Joshua to Israel					
Final counsel by Joshua to Israel					

Figure 13

Him. Take, for instance, the crossing of the Jordan in chapter 3. " 'As soon as the priests who carry the ark of the LORD—the Lord of all the earth—set foot in the Jordan, the water flowing downstream will be cut off and stand up in a heap' " (v. 13). Read the next four verses in your Bible and observe that, although the word *faith* does not appear in this text, the response of the people and of the priests was an exercise both of faith and of obedience. The same is true with the conquest of Jericho in chapter 6, where the armies of Israel were expected to conquer the city by a method which seemed absurd, but was wholly dependent upon God and in obedience to His specific commands. Hebrews 11:30 gives us the divine commentary on this episode, for there we read, "By faith the walls of Jericho fell, after the people had marched around them for seven days."

Practical Application

The practical application of all this is self-evident. The God who was present with His people as they took possession of the land of Canaan is just as truly present with us today. We read in Hebrews 13:5, " 'Never will I leave you; never will I forsake you.' " And in the closing words of the Great Commission, the Lord Jesus Himself said to His disciples, " 'And surely I will be with you always, to the very end of the age' " (Matthew 28:20).

The book of Joshua also reminds us that God is not only the God who is ever present with His own, but that He is also our mighty, all-powerful God. There may be insurmountable obstacles confronting us and difficulties far too great for us to overcome, just as there were for Joshua and his people. But the Lord, who dried up the waters of the River Jordan and performed miracles in behalf of His own in those ancient times, is just as able to perform great and mighty things for us today.

And the God of Israel who kept His word to His people when they entered the land of promise is also our faithful God who will keep His word to us. The Lord Jesus declared, " 'Heaven and earth will pass away, but my words shall never pass away' " (Matthew 24:35).

As God brought the people of Israel into an experience of temporal blessings because of their faith and obedience, we can come into the enjoyment of spiritual blessings only as we take God at His word and walk in simple obedience to Him. Surely one of the primary lessons of this book of Joshua is that there is no blessing for the disobedient believer. On the other hand, there is glorious victory, abundance, and rest for the child of God who trusts and obeys Him implicitly.

The Final Step

As a final step, we need to title our chart by summing up the contents of the entire book in a brief phrase. We have entitled our chart, "The Occupation of the Land of Canaan by Joshua and the People of Israel." See figure 13.

EXERCISE 7

Even though we have completed a synthetic chart on the book of Joshua, several features in it will be an enigma unless we also approach the book from a geographical, cultural, and historical point of view.

Therefore, as part of your assignment, review these three methods of study. With the help of an atlas, make a map of the land of Canaan, showing the route Joshua took in his campaigns and the cities he conquered. Indicate also the territory which was allotted to each of the twelve tribes.

To learn the cultural and historical background of the book of Joshua, read the following passages: Leviticus 18; Numbers 13, 14, and 32; and Deuteronomy 7:1-6. Once you have considered these passages, consult a Bible dictionary or other reference book for additional information.

As the second part of your assignment, construct a synthetic chart on the book of Judges. Summarize each chapter. (Remember that each chapter does not necessarily end at the chapter divisions indicated in your Bible.) Show the main divisions, the summarization of the main divisions, and the prominent features or distinctives of the book.

8. THE DOCTRINAL APPROACH

Definition of Bible Doctrine

I suppose that most of my readers have read through the first three chapters of Genesis. Even if you have never been to Bible school or had the privilege of any formal training in the study of the Scriptures, simply by reading those first chapters in the Bible you have learned some doctrinal truths.

Some of the truths which crossed your mind while you read may have been like the following. There is a God. He is the creator of the universe. He is omnipotent, performing His acts of creation simply by willing them or speaking. He is an intelligent being, producing His creation in an orderly manner to fulfill purposeful ends. He is the creator of man. Man is made in the image of God. God is sovereign, possessing authority over the universe and over man. Man is free to choose for good or evil. Man was created in innocency. Man fell by an act of his own deliberate choice. Man's sin separated him from the presence of God.

These truths and thousands of others are to be found in the pages of Scripture. Thus, the Bible is our textbook of faith. That is to say, it is what God Himself has shown us we should believe about Him and our relationship to Him and His universe. The Scriptures contain the whole body of truth we are to believe. This corpus of truth is called Bible doctrine. Theology, which literally means "the study of God," is akin to doctrine, and these two terms are often used synonymously.

Forms of Truth Found in Scripture

Indirect Doctrinal Statements

In the Bible, doctrinal truths are found in various forms. Particularly in the historical and prophetical sections of Scripture, we find truth stated indirectly by assumption, implication, or illustration. For example, such important doctrines as God's existence, His personality, and His concern for men are assumptions that are taken for granted in the Bible. The doctrinal statements we discovered from our reading of Genesis were derived by implication from the account of the creation and fall of man in Genesis 1-3. Although the terms *creator, sovereignty, free moral agent,* and *sin* do not appear in the text, these concepts are clearly indicated in the three opening chapters of the Word of God. This is also true of the rest of the Bible where there are countless doctrinal implications of vital importance.

We find numerous examples of illustration in the Bible. For instance, the account of the destruction of Sodom and Gomorrah in Genesis 19 shows forth God's holiness and His righteous retribution upon man because of sin. The familiar story of David and Goliath teaches us the importance of confidence in God's omnipotence in the face of overwhelming odds. And the entire book of Esther, where God's name is not even mentioned once, is an outstanding picture of the providence of God in which we see Him looking ahead and making provision for His people from the beginning of the crisis to its end.

Explicit Doctrinal Statements

Scattered throughout the Bible we also find hundreds of explicit doctrinal statements. For instance, in the following quotation from Exodus 34:6-7, we have a specific expression of the character of God. "And he [the LORD] passed in front of Moses, proclaiming, 'The LORD, the LORD, the compassionate and gracious God, slow to anger, abounding in love and faithfulness, maintaining love to thousands, and forgiving wickedness, rebellion and sin. Yet he does not leave the guilty unpunished; he punishes the childen and their children for the sin of the fathers to the third and fourth generations.' "

In Deuteronomy 6:4 we find an explicit declaration of monotheism: "Hear, O Israel: The LORD our God, the LORD is one."

The Psalms contain a great number of direct statements of doctrine. One such statement occurs in Psalm 19:8: "The precepts of the LORD are right, giving joy to the heart. The commands of the LORD are radiant, giving light to the eyes."

In the major prophets we find Isaiah 53:6, which speaks of the lost condition of man: "We all, like sheep, have gone astray, each of us has turned to his own way; and the LORD has laid on him the iniquity of us all."

In the minor prophets, Malachi 3:6 speaks of the immutability of God: "I the LORD do not change."

We also find examples of explicit doctrinal statements in the New Testament. One, John 3:16, is one of the most familiar salvation texts in the Bible: "For God so loved the world that he gave his one and only Son, that whoever believes in him shall not perish but have eternal life."

One last quotation, another salvation text, is from 1 Peter 3:18: "For Christ died for sins once for all, the righteous for the unrighteous, to bring you to God."

All these statements and many others throughout the Bible which are just as clearly stated enable us to learn what the Bible teaches concerning the fundamentals of our faith.

Doctrinal Words and Phrases

Besides indirect and explicit doctrinal statements, there are hundreds upon hundreds of single words or phrases in the Bible which are distinctively doctrinal in character. Our understanding of these words and phrases often has an important bearing upon our knowledge of doctrine.

Here are just a few examples of doctrinal words and phrases: law, grace, peace, faith, works, cross, justification, redemption, gift, carnal, separation, kingdom of God, works of the flesh, in Christ, the Lord of Hosts, the Spirit of Truth, the sanctification of the Spirit.

Extended Doctrinal Passages

Some portions of the Bible are predominantly doctrinal in substance. That is, they are a systematic presentation of a particular important doctrinal theme.

For example, the apostle Paul's epistle to the Romans contains an extended treatise on the righteousness of God in the gospel. Beginning with Romans 1:18, Paul discusses condemnation, or man's need for righteousness. From 3:21-5:21 he presents justification, or how God accounts us as righteous. Beginning with 6:1, Paul discusses sanctification, or the impartation of righteousness. And in 8:14-39 he concludes with glorification, or the final realization of righteousness.

There are other portions of the Bible, most of them much shorter than the one above, which consist of a special delineation of some vital truth. These are found in most of Paul's epistles, in the letters by Peter and John, and in the epistle to the Hebrews.

The Main Doctrines of the Bible

Since the beginning of the Christian era, eminent scholars have given much thought to the doctrines found in the Bible. Many of these scholars have spent a lifetime studying theology, carefully examining in context all biblical passages relating to every doctrine in the Scriptures. They have then arranged the material they have gathered, and placed it in nine major categories as follows:

Bibliology, the study of the character of the Bible.

Theology proper or theism, which includes the study of God's attributes or characteristics, names, and works.

Christology, or the study of the person of Christ.

Pneumatology, the doctrine of the Holy Spirit.

Angelology, or what the Bible teaches about angels, both holy and fallen, and about Satan.

Anthropology, or the study of the origin, nature, and fall of man, and his present responsibility and destiny.

Soteriology, the doctrine of salvation.

Ecclesiology, the doctrine of the church as the spiritual body of believers.

Eschatology, or the study of the final events in the history of Israel, the Gentiles, and the church; and the eternal state of all things.

Each one of these categories is broken down into various subdivisions. For example, soteriology, the study of the doctrine of salvation, is divided into categories such as the nature of Christ's atoning sacrifice; redemption, or the payment of ransom for sin; justification; regeneration, or the new birth; sanctification; and other categories. This codification of the doctrines of the Bible is called systematic theology. All of the great fundamentals of the faith have been so well organized in textbooks on Bible doctrine, or systematic theology, that the average reader can now easily gain a comprehensive view of biblical truth.

Procedure for a Doctrinal Study in a Book of the Bible

The field of doctrinal study is so rich and so vast that no one has ever been able to discover all there is to know about biblical truth. The ability to study intelligently an extended doctrinal passage in a book calls for exegetical and expositional skills which are beyond our scope to teach here. However, by a simple method, which can be described as a topical collation of the doctrinal materials contained in a book, it is possible to have the delightful experience of doing doctrinal research on your own. Let's put this procedure into practice using what is by now a very familiar book—1 Thessalonians.

1. Select the area of doctrine you wish to study in a single book of the Bible.

To choose which area of doctrine to study, begin by reading and re-reading the book you are studying. As you read, note the major doctrinal areas the author touches upon in his book. For example, you may read 1 Thessalonians and decide to study the Christology found in it; that is, all that its five chapters have to say about the person of Christ. If you should attempt to do this you will find that it is a much bigger task than you had imagined. The book deals with the following doctrinal features relative to the person of Christ: His relationship to God the Father, His death and resurrection, His relationship to the gospel, His second coming as it relates to the believer and the world, His relationship to the Christian, and His titles.

It is obvious that it will be necessary for you to limit your research to a narrower area. For instance, you might restrict your doctrinal investigation to the effects which the second coming of Christ will have on the believer as shown in 1 Thessalonians. Or you may choose to concentrate on the titles given to Christ in this epistle.

We shall pursue the latter topic in our study in this chapter.

2. Make a chart listing every occurrence in the book of the item which is the subject of your doctrinal research.

The genius of the topical collation of doctrinal material is to note every item in the book which relates to the subject under investigation. As we proceed with our research, you may be surprised to find how many references to the titles of Christ this brief letter by Paul contains. In the chart below we have set down in parallel columns every single reference to a name of Christ in this epistle, showing the numerical order, scripture reference, and a portion of the text showing which title of Christ appears.

No.	Reference	Quotation
	**Titles of Christ in 1 Thessalonians**
1	1:1	To the church ... in God the Father and the *Lord Jesus Christ*
2	1:1	Grace and peace to you from ... the *Lord Jesus Christ*
3	1:3	... endurance inspired by hope in our *Lord Jesus Christ*
4	1:6	You became imitators of us and of the *Lord*
5	1:8	The *Lord's* message rang out ...
6	1:10	... and to wait for his *Son* from heaven ...
7	1:10	... whom he raised from the dead—*Jesus*....
8	2:7	As apostles of *Christ*....
9	2:14	... became imitators of God's churches in Judea, which are in *Christ Jesus*....
10	2:15	... who killed the *Lord Jesus*....
11	2:19	... in which we will glory in the presence of our *Lord Jesus*....
12	3:2	... God's fellow worker in spreading the gospel of *Christ*....
13	3:8	... since you are standing firm in the *Lord*.
14	3:11	Now may our God and Father himself and our *Lord Jesus* clear the way....
15	3:12	May the *Lord* make your love increase....
16	3:13	... when our *Lord Jesus* comes with all his holy ones.
17	4:1	... and urge you in the *Lord Jesus*....
18	4:2	... instructions we gave you by the authority of the *Lord Jesus*.
19	4:6	The *Lord* will punish men for all such sins....
20	4:14	We believe that *Jesus* died and rose again....
21	4:14	... God will bring with *Jesus*....
22	4:15	According to the *Lord's* own word....
23	4:15	... who are left till the coming of the *Lord*....
24	4:16	For the *Lord* himself will come down....
25	4:16	... and the dead in *Christ* will rise first.
26	4:17	... to meet the *Lord* in the air.
27	4:17	And so we will be with the *Lord* forever.
28	5:2	... the day of the *Lord* will come like a thief....
29	5:9	... to receive salvation through our *Lord Jesus Christ*.
30	5:12	... who are over you in the *Lord*....
31	5:18	... this is God's will for you in *Christ Jesus*.
32	5:23	... at the coming of our *Lord Jesus Christ*.
33	5:27	I charge you before the *Lord*....
34	5:28	The grace of our *Lord Jesus Christ* be with you.

3. Codify the material you have gathered together.

Organize the information which you have obtained by placing it in appropriate order. The sequence which you use may be logical, chronological, numerical, or some other arrangement which is best suited to the material you have at hand. By going over all the titles given to Christ in 1 Thessalonians we have found that the Apostle Paul referred to Christ thirty-four times by name in the five brief chapters which make up the epistle, and he gave seven different titles to our Savior. We have listed these titles in order of frequency.

> Son—one time
> Christ Jesus—two times
> Jesus—three times
> Christ—three times
> Lord Jesus—six times
> Lord Jesus Christ—six times
> Lord—thirteen times

4. Learn the significance of your observations.

With the help of any extra-biblical tools which may be available to you, try to learn the significance of the material you have assembled together. The footnotes in the Scofield Reference Bible contain helpful information on some of the basic doctrines, and if you possess an edition of this Bible you will have no difficulty in locating the proper footnotes by checking the index of references in the back of the Bible.

Using the Scofield Reference Bible, Strong's concordance, Bible dictionaries, and other sources, we have discovered the following facts about three of the titles of the Lord Jesus used in 1 Thessalonians.

Christ. Christ is the Greek form of the Hebrew *Messiah,* which means "anointed." Three classes of individuals in Old Testament times were anointed with oil: prophets, priests, and kings. Christ, who is *the* prophet, *the* priest, and *the* king, was anointed with the Holy Spirit (Matthew 3:16) to show that He was indeed the anointed one of God, the fulfillment in His Person of the Old Testament promises of a coming prophet (Deuteronomy 18:15-19), priest (Psalm 110:4), and king (2 Samuel 7:7-10). Thus, *Christ* is the New Testament equivalent to the Hebrew title *Messiah,* just as Andrew said to his brother Simon in John 1:41, " 'We have found the Messiah' (that is, the Christ)."

Jesus. Jesus is the Greek form of the Hebrew name *Jehoshua* or

Joshua, which literally means "Jehovah the savior" (Luke 1:31, 2:21). This is the human name for our Lord and relates Him to the great purpose of His coming into the world—to save mankind from sin (Matthew 1:21).

Lord. Although the term *Lord,* meaning "master," is used occasionally in the New Testament to refer to humans, it is most often employed in reference to Christ. (See Colossians 4:1 where the very same word is applied both to man and to Christ.) The New Testament writers used *Lord* repeatedly as the divine title of Jesus Christ (Acts 2:36; Romans 1:3, 4; Philippians 2:11). It is also used specifically in the New Testament to refer to the Jehovah of the Old Testament. (Note the following references in which the title *Lord* is used in relation to the Jehovah of the Old Testament: Matthew 1:22, 23; 3:3; Mark 12:29, 30; Luke 1:68; 2:9. Also observe how the following references identify Jesus Christ with Jehovah Himself: Matthew 22:43-45; John 8:58; 14:8-10; 20:28; Acts 9:5.)

5. *Examine the relationship to the context of the doctrinal features you are studying.*

Investigation of the relationship of the context to any part of Scripture you are studying is always important. However, in the type of doctrinal research we are doing, that is, topical collation of doctrinal material, the beginner may not find it practical to attempt it. This is particularly true in the case of 1 Thessalonians with its many references to Christ's various titles. However, we can consider in a general way the relationship of 1 Thessalonians to our doctrinal study of the titles of Christ and obtain some new insights into spiritual truth.

As we have noted in previous chapters, the contents and historical background of 1 Thessalonians clearly indicate that the church in Thessalonica was composed of both Jews and Gentiles, all of whom had recently come to know the Lord Jesus. Almost immediately after their salvation they had been thrown into the crucible of persecution by Jews who bitterly opposed the gospel message. It is evident from 3:1-5 that at the time this letter was written these young Christians were continuing to endure great suffering for their faith. To the new Jewish Christians in particular, then, the Lord's name would bear special significance when Paul wrote of Him as *Christ,* their long-looked-for Messiah. To the new Gentile believers the name *Jesus,* Jehovah who came down from heaven to save men from sin, would have been much more meaningful. But to Jews and Gentiles together He was known as Jesus Christ or Christ Jesus, in whom the hope of Jew and Gentile for salvation was met and blended.

Paul's frequent use of the term *Lord* demands our special attention, however, because this title is employed more often than any other in the epistle. Looking at our chart we observe that *Lord,* together with the title with which it is used in combination, *Lord Jesus,* or *Lord Jesus Christ,* is employed particularly in connection with the suffering of the believers in Thessalonica. Perhaps the Apostle used this term to remind these suffering saints that their fiery trials did not come by accident, they were not merely the victims of wicked men, but their blessed Lord who was in ultimate control of all things was permitting them their present trials so that He might "strengthen [their] hearts so that [they] will be blameless and holy in the presence of our God and Father when our Lord Jesus comes with all his holy ones" (3:13).

We observe, too, that the term *Lord* also appears in conjunction with the second coming of Christ. He said when He was upon this earth, "And if I go and prepare a place for you, I will come back and take you to be with me that you also may be where I am" (John 14:3). It would seem, then, that when Paul applied this title to the return of Christ for His own, he was assuring the Thessalonian believers—and all the saints who have read this epistle since that time—that nothing can prevent our sovereign Lord from fulfilling His promise to take His own to be with Himself. Note 1 Thessalonians 4:16, 17: "For the Lord himself will come down from heaven, with a loud command, with the voice of the archangel and with the trumpet call of God, and the dead in Christ will rise first. After that, we who are still alive and are left will be caught up with them in the clouds to meet the Lord in the air. And so we will be with the Lord forever."

By observing the context in which the combined title *Lord Jesus Christ* appears, we discover that the possessive personal pronoun *our* immediately precedes five out of the seven occurrences of this combination of titles. Thus, Paul emphasized throughout the epistle the personal relationship which both he and his readers had with the Lord. He was not only *the* Lord Jesus Christ, but *their* Lord Jesus Christ, with a vital, personal, and blessed relationship with them.

Finally, as we look once more through the epistle we observe that of the eighty-nine verses that compose the letter, one in three contains a reference to Christ by title. Thus, by constantly and repeatedly men-

tioning the Savior by name, Paul seems to have sought to get these
young converts to fix their eyes upon Jesus.

6. *Make practical application of the truths to your own life.*

Having learned fresh insights of truth from your doctrinal studies,
consider ways you might apply these to yourself. To do this, meditate
prayerfully upon the doctrinal truths you have found and pray that the
Lord might reveal areas in your own heart and life to which these truths
need to be directed.

There are many applications that could be made from the doctrinal
study we have just completed on the titles of Christ in 1 Thessalonians.
Here are two we would like to suggest. First, since Jesus is my Lord, I
need to ask myself: Do I really give Him worship? If I do, when and
how do I worship Him? He is worthy of all honor and praise—what
part do I have in giving Him the honor due Him?

Second, Jesus Christ is my personal Lord: Have I truly given Him
His rightful place in my heart and life? Have I fully and totally surren-
dered myself to let Him be the master of my heart and my will?

EXERCISE 8

Although the book of Jonah is predominantly historical in nature, we can
learn a great deal of doctrine from it, too. In fact, the Lord enters so much into
the story of Jonah that if we were to take Him out of the book there would be
little left that is worthwhile to write about. There is so much it contains about
God that we think it best to limit your doctrinal assignment to discovering
what the book of Jonah says about the sovereignty of God by illustration or implication.

To begin, list each reference in the text to God's supreme power and
authority and make a brief notation of how it is illustrated or implied. Follow
the directions contained in this chapter to complete your investigation of this
doctrinal subject in Jonah.

9. THE TOPICAL APPROACH

Definition of the Topical Method

The topical approach to Bible study is the method of selecting a given subject in the Bible and tracing the occurrences of that subject in relation to its context. The topic may consist of a concept, a theme, a word, or a phrase which occurs in a book; it might also be in a portion of a book, a section of the Bible like the Pentateuch, the Minor Prophets, or Paul's pastoral epistles, and possibly throughout the entire Old Testament or the New Testament.

Topical study is not made from the occurrences of a subject in a single paragraph or two. It is derived from a repetition of a concept, word, or phrase widely scattered throughout a large portion of Scripture. When the topic is doctrinal in nature and we trace through the occurrences of the doctrinal concept, the study becomes a doctrinal one.

Variety of Topical Studies

The Scriptures offer an inexhaustible storehouse of materials for topical study, and the topics cover every conceivable subject relating to man and to his needs. Here in this storehouse of topics we may discover such subjects as: duties of parenthood, responsibilities of believers to the state, pledges which God makes to His children, conditions of blessing, blunders of God's saints, opportunities for reaching the lost, cornerstones of character, steps in discipleship, foregleams of heaven, the wiles of Satan, spiritual sacrifices, the joys of witnessing for Christ, secrets of victory in the Christian life. All these topics and hundreds more are to be found in the pages of the Bible awaiting our discovery and research.

Before we go on to the discussion of the study of a topic in a given book, let us look at a few examples of topical studies from a wide range of Bible content.

The first example draws its material from various portions of the New Testament. This one we entitle "Privileges Which Each One of Us May Experience."

1. The privilege of becoming a child of God, John 1:12.
2. The privilege of becoming an heir of God, Romans 8:16, 17.
3. The privilege of becoming a disciple of Christ, John 8:31.
4. The privilege of becoming a friend of Christ, John 15:13-15.
5. The privilege of becoming a laborer together with God, 1 Corinthians 3:9.

A second illustration is drawn from the Old Testament and consists of various observations about sweet things found in the Old Testament Scriptures. Observe that this topic does not deal with all the sweet things referred to in the first main.portion of the Bible, but only with some of the prominent sweet things in the Old Testament.

1. A sweet savor offering. Genesis 8:20, 21; Leviticus 1:9, 13, 17—foreshadowing the sacrifice of Christ which was to God an offering of a sweet smelling savor. See also Ephesians 5:2.
2. Sweet waters. Exodus 15:25—illustrating the way in which the Lord is able to turn the bitter experiences of life into sweetness for us.
3. Sweet words. Psalm 119:103—suggesting the sweetness of the Word of God to the believer who is in vital touch with him.
4. Sweet fruit. Song of Solomon 2:3—possibly indicating the delight the believer has in the person and work of Christ for him.
5. Sweet voice. Song of Solomon 2:14—possibly symbolizing the pleasure which Christ the heavenly bridegroom has in hearing the voice of a member of His bride, the Church, whenever the believer addresses Him in prayer and in praise. Compare Ephesians 5:25-27.

We draw yet another illustration from Old Testament references.

Selecting the topic, Men in Whom God Delights, we discover with the help of a concordance certain kinds of people in whom God delights.

1. God delights in upright men, Proverbs 11:20.
2. God delights in God-fearing men, Psalm 147:11.
3. God delights in obedient men, 1 Samuel 15:22.
4. God delights in truthful men, Proverbs 12:22.

A fourth illustration is based on both the Old and the New Testament. This is entitled "Important Bible Gardens."

1. The Garden of Eden. Genesis 2:15; 3:1, 17-24—where man was condemned to death because of sin.
2. The Garden of Gethsemane. John 18:1; Matthew 26:36-42—where Christ accepted the cup of divine wrath because of man's sin.
3. The Garden where Christ was buried. John 19:14, 42—where Christ lay in death because of man's sin.
4. The Garden relating to the new Jerusalem. Revelation 22:1-3 —where there will be no more death and no more sin.

The fourth example is also drawn from the Old and the New Testaments. We entitle this "Significant Storms at Sea."

1. The storm which wrecked the ships built by Jehoshaphat to gather gold contrary to the word of God. 1 Kings 22:48; Deuteronomy 17:17.
2. The storm which came upon the ship in which Jonah sought to flee from the presence of the Lord. Jonah 1:3, 4.
3. The storm which befell the disciples when they set out across the Sea of Galilee in obedience to the word of the Lord. Mark 4: 35-41.
4. The storm which befell the apostle Paul on his way to Rome to witness before Caesar. Acts 27.

If a topic is based on a large section of the Scriptures and the references to that particular subject are very numerous, it will be necessary either to narrow down the topic or to omit consideration of some of the references to it.

With the permission of its author, Dr. Willard M. Aldrich, President Emeritus of Multnomah School of the Bible, we have borrowed our next example of a topical outline from the "Doorstep Evangel." This outline, which is built upon the topic Reasons for the Christian to Be Happy, lists a few of the reasons, based upon Scripture, for the Christian's happiness.

1. The Christian has acceptance.
   (1) With God, John 6:37, Luke 15:2, Ephesians 1:6-7 KJV.
   (2) With fellow Christians, 1 John 1:7.
   (3) With a renewed self, Romans 8:29-30, 12:1-2.
2. The Christian's burden of guilt is gone.
   (1) Through the forgiveness of his sins, Isaiah 1:18, Ephesians 1:6-7.
   (2) Through his justification by God, Acts 13:38-39, Romans 5:1.
3. The Christian finds purpose in life.
   (1) In doing the will of God, Romans 12:1-2.
   (2) In living for the glory of God, Colossians 3:17, 1 Corinthians 15:58.
4. The Christian has a workable formula for happiness.
   (1) Through a right relationship with God, Psalm 16:8, 11.
   (2) Through a right relationship with his fellow men, Galatians 5:13-14, 6:10.
   (3) Through a right relationship to things, Acts 20:35.
5. The Christian has a happy prospect beyond the grave.
   (1) To be with the Lord forever, Psalm 23:6.
   (2) To be satisfied when he awakes with the Lord's likeness, Psalm 17:15.

The last two examples are each drawn from a single book of the Bible. The first of these is based on the book of Revelation, and draws attention to several white things mentioned in that book.

1. White hair. 1:14—an emblem of purity. Compare Psalm 51:7.
2. A white stone. 2:17—a token of fellowship.
3. White raiment. 3:5; 6:11; 7:9—a garment of righteousness.
4. A white cloud. 14:14, 16—a foreboding of judgment.

  5. A white horse. 19:11—a symbol of victory.
  6. A great white throne. 20:11—a judgment of justice.

Our last example of a topical study drawn from a single book in the Bible is "God's Standards for the Church" based on the book of Acts.

  1. It should be a united church, Acts 1:14; 2:1, 46; 4:24, 32; 5:12.
  2. It should be a Spirit-filled church, Acts 4:8, 31; 6:3, 5; 7:58; 9:17; 11:24; 13:4.
  3. It should be a praying church, Acts 1:14; 4:24-31; 6:4; 10:9; 12:5, 12.
  4. It should be a witnessing church, Acts 1:8; 4:18-20, 33; 5:27-29; 8:5; 26:22.
  5. It should be a missionary-minded church, Acts 13:1-4; 14:27; 15:36-40; 18:18-23.

Procedure for the Study of a Topic in a Book in the Bible

1. Regard every topic in the Bible as important.

Every topic has been placed in the Scriptures by the Divine Author to meet the needs of mankind in every circumstance of life. And what might appear at first sight to be trivial may suggest truths of the utmost importance. Furthermore, if it is important for us to know what great men have said on a certain subject, how much more important it is for us to know what God Himself has written or said on a given subject.

2. Select a general subject in the book and then limit your study to a particular aspect of that subject.

We may find numerous subjects in every book of the Bible. But, if we deal with too general of a subject, we may find ourselves faced with a task greater than our abilities. It is therefore best for the beginner to narrow his investigation.

For example, the book of Proverbs abounds in interesting subjects. There we find repeated reference to the wise man and to wisdom. The friend, a neighbor, the talebearer, the young man, the diligent man, the father, the mother, the son, and the fool are other topics. For instance, the word "fool" or its equivalent occurs more than eighty times in the book in the King James Version. If we had the space it would be

valuable to go through every one of these references and examine them
to see what this book teaches on the subject. We could simplify our
task by taking a certain aspect of the subject, leaving the investigation
of its other aspects to a later time.

For instance, we could limit our study to one of the following topics
in relation to the fool: the characteristics of a fool, the pleasures of a
fool, the lips of a fool, the attitudes of a fool toward his parents, the
troubles which fools bring upon others.

Now turn to the book of Jonah and look at a number of specific
topics found in this book.

1. Great events in the book.
2. Contrasts in the book.
3. Unique instruments which God used.
4. Object lessons in the book.
5. Miracles in the book.
6. Types of prayer in the book.
7. Lessons on prayer drawn from the book.

*3. Make a list of every occurrence of your topic in the order in which it
   appears in the book by noting every reference to it.*

You will thereby learn everything that God has to say in the book on
that particular subject. If the topic consists of the investigation of a
fixed word or phrase, use an unabridged concordance or *Nave's Topical Bible* to run down each occurrence of the item in the order in which
it occurs.

For example, if we select the first of the topics from the book of
Jonah which we mentioned in the preceding paragraph, we would
have the following list: 1:2—the great city of Nineveh; 1:4—A great
wind; 1:12—A great storm; 1:17—A great fish; 3:2—the great city of
Nineveh; 3:3—Nineveh was a very large city; it took three days to go
all through it; 4:2—you are a gracious and compassionate God slow to
anger and abounding (or great—KJV) in love; 4:11—Nineveh . . . that
great city.

If, on the other hand, your topic consists of a concept rather than a
fixed word or phrase, we shall need to carefully look through and list
every reference where the general idea appears. Making use once
more of the book of Jonah, we select "the miracles in the book" as our
example.

Although the word "miracle" does not occur a single time in its four chapters, there are several outstanding miracles recorded in the book of Jonah. 1:4, 12, 15—The miracle of the storm, both in the way in which the storm began and in the way in which it ended. 1:17—The miracle of the great fish. 2:1, 10—The miracle of Jonah's preservation. 3:5-10—The miracle of the repentance of the great city of Nineveh. 4:6-8—The miracle of the gourd or vine.

4. Classify the material you have assembled together.

This means arranging the information which we have obtained in some kind of an appropriate order. The order we use may be numerical, chronological, logical, comparative, contrastive, or some other form depending upon the purpose we have in mind for our study.

For example, the words *conscience* or *consciences* appear over thirty times in *Strong's Unabridged Concordance*. In order to classify the material we gather together from this source on the conscience, we can set it forth under two categories. First, types of an unsatisfactory conscience: weak, 1 Corinthians 8:7, 12; seared, 1 Timothy 4:2; defiled, Titus 1:15; evil, Hebrews 10:22. Types of a satisfactory conscience: purged, Hebrews 9:14; good, Acts 23:1, Hebrews 13:8; pure, 1 Timothy 3:9; inoffensive, Acts 24:16.

In connection with the example shown above, the great things in the book of Jonah, the most suitable classification in this case would be to note the numerical order of the items. Thus we see that the greatness of the city of Nineveh is referred to in the book four times, whereas every other item is referred to only once.

5. If at all possible, learn the meaning of each occurrence of your topic.

In order to do this it will be necessary for you to use whatever extra-biblical tools are available to you. Insofar as the study of a fixed word or phrase is concerned, an unabridged concordance or *Vine's Expository Dictionary of New Testament Words* would be especially helpful.

In connection with the "good" conscience referred to under the last rule, it is important to note that the writers of the New Testament used two different Greek adjectives to qualify the term "conscience." One of these words, *agathos,* is used most frequently in the New Testament to speak about a good conscience. It has reference to goodness according to the standard of that which is right. This usage is employed in

Acts 23:1; 1 Timothy 1:5, 19; 1 Peter 3:16. The other Greek word, *kalos,* has reference to goodness according to the standard of beauty and is employed in Hebrews 13:8.

The word *great* in the book of Jonah appears eight times in the King James Version of the Bible. Seven times it is derived from a Hebrew word implying something large. The one instance where the word great has a different connotation in the original text than the other references is in 4:2 and it reads, "Thou art a gracious God, and merciful, slow to anger and of great kindness," and has the implication of abundance. Thus, the New International Version of the Bible translates the same reference as, "You are a gracious and compassionate God, slow to anger and abounding in love."

6. Note the relationship of the usages of your topic to their context.

Whenever part of Scripture is taken from its context—that is, the surrounding words, sentences, paragraphs—the meaning of the text can easily be misunderstood or misconstrued. It is important, therefore, that we observe the context and note the setting in which each use of the topic is found.

In order to illustrate the importance of this step, let us note the setting in which the phrase "great city" occurs in the book. Open your Bible to the book of Jonah and look at the following references: 1:1, 2; 3:1, 2; 4:10, 11. To these, a fourth reference, 3:3, 4, could be added: "Jonah obeyed the word of the LORD and went to Nineveh. Now Nineveh was a very large city; it took three days to go all through it. Jonah started into the city, going a day's journey, and he proclaimed: 'Forty more days and Nineveh will be destroyed.' "

In three of the four instances where there is reference to a great or large city, it is the Lord Himself who describes the city in this way to His servant. The fourth reference finds Jonah himself moving a full day's journey into the city.

A study of the context shows, therefore, that the Lord Himself impressed upon Jonah directly His concern for the great city and the importance of the commission that He had entrusted to His servant. It seems that Jonah never really comprehended the mind and purpose of God for this Gentile metropolis. In fact, his petulant demand that the Lord take away his life because he could not have his own way indicates how far removed he was from the heart of God.

Look at the context of the phrase "abounding in love" in 4:2. These were words of none other than Jonah himself. A further study shows that Jonah had a clear knowledge of the character of God. If we compare Jonah's concept of the Lord with the statements in other portions of the divine oracles written prior to the time of the prophet, we would see that Jonah was thoroughly orthodox in his views. Also, his estimate of the Lord's mercy and grace were entirely consistent with the character of God as revealed in those portions of the Old Testament. But the man who spoke so correctly of the Lord's loving character and of His abundant mercy, and who rightly understood his mission to Nineveh as a mission of mercy, was unwilling in his own heart to undertake that mission.

The concluding observation of this context reveals the character of the prophet as one who, though thoroughly orthodox in his doctrine, was willfully out of line with the heart and will of God.

7. *Consider the application to your own life of the truths which you have learned from your topical study.*

As in every other step of Bible study, we need here to look to the Spirit of God. He and He alone can reveal to us how the truths seen in our study should be applied to our own lives. Sometimes the lessons He has to teach us may be by way of conviction and rebuke. Other lessons may be in the form of encouragement and hope. Still others may bring us into His presence to bow in humble worship and praise to our great God and Savior.

We conclude this study with two applications. If Jonah had failed to comprehend God's purpose even though the Lord spoke clearly and repeatedly to him, is it not possible that I, too, may fail to recognize the Lord's will for me although His purpose may be plainly revealed to me in His Word? How I need, therefore, to live close to Him, and be quick to recognize His voice and discern His will. "Renew my life according to your word" (Psalm 119:25). If Jonah, a servant of the Lord who was orthodox in his views of God and knew much about God's loving character, failed to see himself by contrast as a hard, self-willed, and unloving individual, is it not possible for me likewise to be totally blind to my own faults? How important, then, it is for me to lay myself open to the Lord daily that He might reveal through His Word my own shortcomings. How honestly I should plead with David, "Search me, O God, and know my heart; test me, and know my anxious thoughts. See if there is any offensive way in me, and lead me in the way everlasting" (Psalm 139:23, 24).

EXERCISE 9

Doing topical studies on books in the Bible is a process to be learned; it is not picked up by reading one chapter in a book. You must do a topical study all on your own. If you are earnest in your desire to learn, the Lord will help you do a topical study. This may be just a beginning for many more wonderful discoveries of blessed truths.

We suggest that you begin by taking up a topic in 1 Thessalonians and developing it along the lines we have outlined in this chapter. Here are two or three suggested topics to be found in this epistle: responsibilities which Christians have toward one another; patterns from the believers in Thessalonica which we should follow today; lessons we can learn from the epistle about affliction.

For a more extensive treatment of the topical approach in the study of the Bible, see Chapter 1, "The Topical Sermon," in my book, *How to Prepare Bible Messages*.

10. THE PRACTICAL APPROACH

In the previous chapters we have primarily discussed factual material in the Scriptures. The nature of the various approaches to Bible study we have taken up until now has made it necessary to concentrate on facts—and it has been indispensable to our knowledge of the Word of God. However, if you have been alert you may have noticed that from time to time we made certain statements derived from the text and presented them in the form of principles or timeless truths.

Principles based upon the data contained in the Bible may be drawn from every part of the Scriptures and await our observation and discovery. But before we go any further, let us consider carefully what is meant by a principle.

Definition of a Principle

The dictionary defines a principle as a general or fundamental truth, a rule of conduct by which an individual directs his life or actions, or a statement of a basic, true generalization or fact. In other words, a principle is a clear, declarative sentence which is intended to serve as a guide for conduct or procedure.

Let us consider this definition carefully. It teaches us that a principle has several features:

1. It is an assertion or positive statement and not a negative one.
2. It is a clear or incisive declaration, expressed in a single, brief sentence containing one essential idea.
3. It is a truth which is always valid.
4. It is an established rule which is basic for life and conduct.

Every Christian knows that Scripture contains truths, both implicitly and explicitly stated, by which he must order his life. This is one of the features of the Bible which gives it such supreme value over all other literature. When we derive moral or spiritual truths from the centuries-old historical facts in the Scriptures, we relate the Word of God to our times and show its relevance to life today. But timeless principles differ from personal application. Principles are truths which are valid for everyone, whereas personal application relates truth to a specific individual on a specific matter.

Examples of Principles Drawn from Scripture

To illustrate principles which are derived or based upon Scripture, we shall quote a verse and then state a principle we have drawn from this text.

Genesis 15:1. "After this, the word of the LORD came to Abram in a vision: 'Do not be afraid, Abram. I am your shield, your very great reward.' "

Principle: The promise of the Lord's protection is a sufficient guarantee for the believer's safety. Another principle based on the same text: A believer's confidence rests upon the unfailing promises of God.

Psalm 84:11. "For the LORD God is a sun and shield; the LORD bestows favor and honor; no good thing does he withhold from those whose walk is blameless."

Principle: The Lord promises wonderful blessing to those who do His will. A second principle: We experience the Lord's gracious care of us when we walk in obedience to Him.

Matthew 9:37, 38. "Then he said to his disciples, 'The harvest is plentiful but the workers are few. Ask the Lord of the harvest, therefore, to send out workers into his harvest field.' "

Principle: Prayer is the divine method of raising recruits for the Lord's work. Second principle: The prayerful support of the missionary enterprise is the responsibility of God's people at home.

Philippians 2:30. "He [Epaphroditus] almost died for the work of Christ, risking his life to make up for the help you could not give me."

Principle: Whole-hearted dedication to Christ will cause us to disregard our own interests to minister to others. Second principle: Self-sacrifice is the hallmark of a devoted servant of Christ.

If you have read these statements carefully you will note that every one of them possesses the qualifications of a principle we have given above, and is valid to life situations today.

Effects of Deriving Principles from the Scriptures

The exercise of deriving principles has many benefits to the Bible student. First, it obliges us to give careful thought to the text. Simply reading through a Scripture passage will not enable us to see its relevance and the moral or spiritual lessons which lie beneath its surface. But when we begin to think in terms of principles when we are studying our Bibles, we find it becomes necessary for us to know not only what the Bible says and what it means, but what it means to us. This cannot be done by hasty consideration of the text. Instead, it requires prayerful and careful meditation upon the passage. We must ask ourselves how the Scriptural truths are related to life, to our own individual situations, and to those of people around us. Having considered the historical data contained in the Word of God in this light, we must then express our ideas in the form of principles or timeless truths.

Obviously, the more accurately we are able to interpret the Scriptures through effective Bible study methods and exegesis, the more we shall be able to determine the true meaning of the text. The techniques discussed in previous chapters, when put into practice, will make possible the formulation of many valid principles from Scripture.

Inasmuch as we have centered most of our Bible study in the book of Jonah, we shall demonstrate by drawing principles from the first few verses of the first chapter of Jonah. To gain the maximum benefit from these examples, open your Bible to the book of Jonah and read each verse in the text before noting the following principles derived from them.

Verse 1. The Lord deals sovereignly with each one of His people. The Lord speaks to us through His Word.

Verse 2. The Lord observes the evil which men do upon this earth. God is the moral governor of mankind.

Verse 3. The easy way is not always the right way. We pay a price every time we disobey the Lord.

Verse 4. The Lord has ways of catching up with a man who tries to run away from Him. God uses even the elements to fulfill His purposes.

Verse 5. A disobedient believer is often totally insensitive to the needs of those around him. A child of God who is out of His will can bring much trouble to others besides himself.

Verse 6. The Lord sometimes employs the unsaved to awaken a disobedient believer to his responsibility. When a believer is out of the will of God he becomes a poor testimony to the unsaved.

Verse 7. The Lord can use unexpected means to bring His rebellious child to task. We never know how soon sin will find us out.

The exercise of deriving principles also obliges us to think in terms of ideas which are embedded in the text. As you have no doubt discovered by comparing the Scripture verses we have quoted with the principles we have formulated from them, the truths we have stated are not a mere repetition of the words of the text. Instead, they are concepts which have resulted from noting what is either stated explicitly or implied by the words of the text.

For example, the principle, "the Lord promises wonderful blessing to those who do His will," is drawn from what Psalm 84:11 states distinctly: "No good thing does he withhold from those whose walk is blameless." Again, the principle, "Prayer is the divine method for raising recruits for the Lord's work," is based upon the plainly expressed statement of Christ in Matthew 9:38: "Ask the Lord of the harvest, therefore, to send out workers into his harvest field."

On the other hand, the principle, "the prayerful support of the missionary enterprise is a responsibility of God's people at home," is an implication; that is to say, it is not based on an explicit statement found in Matthew 9:38, but is an idea which is suggested by or indicated indirectly by the text. The same is true of all the principles we have formulated from the text in Jonah 1:1-7.

Procedure for the Determination of Principles

1. Do your best to obtain the correct interpretation of the text before attempting to derive principles from it.

We cannot emphasize too strongly that an accurate understanding of the text is basic to the derivation of correct principles from Scripture. If we misunderstand the meaning of the text, we are in danger of drawing conclusions wholly contrary to the meaning of the sacred writings and we may be misled into all sorts of devious ways.

Sometimes a text may seem to have a specific meaning to us, but in reality applies only to the particular situation referred to in the Bible.

Take, for instance, the instructions Jesus gave to the disciples in Matthew 10:9, 10 as He sent them out to preach: "Do not take along any gold or silver or copper in your belts; take no bag for the journey, or extra tunic, or sandals or a staff." Some may deduce from these verses that whenever a servant of the Lord goes out into Christian service he should take nothing of a temporal nature along with him. A careful consideration of the passages from which these words are taken, however, will show that what the Lord was seeking to impress upon His disciples was the urgency of their commission. Theirs was a work which necessitated immediate and undivided attention.

In the same way, some of the promises of the Bible must be considered in the light of their individual, cultural, or dispensational setting. The dispensational setting can often be ascertained by observation of the context and comparison of parallel Scripture references. For instance, in 2 Samuel 7:16 the Lord made the following promise to David: "Your house and your kingdom will endure forever before me; your throne will be established forever." The context and various cross references such as Psalm 89:30-37, Luke 1:31-33, and Acts 2:29-36 clearly indicate that this promise given to David would be and could be fulfilled only in one of his descendants who would be eternal; namely, his Son, the Lord Jesus Christ, who will live forever, and whose throne will be an everlasting throne.

We wish, therefore, to point out that although it is not possible to discuss here the basic principles of Biblical interpretation, one of the most important principles of interpretation is always to consider the text in relation to its context.

2. *See to it that every principle you enunciate is in keeping with the teaching of the Word of God.*

If any statement you make as a principle is contrary to the Scriptures, then it cannot be a valid truth. Therefore, as you attempt to formulate principles, make sure that each moral and spiritual lesson is wholly in accord with God's Word. As a beginner, you may find it wise to check with a more mature Christian who has a sound knowledge of the Scriptures to determine if the principles you have derived are in accord with what the Bible teaches. It is possible that what appears at first sight to be a command or the right kind of procedure for a Christian to follow may not necessarily be in accordance with the divine will as it is revealed in the entire Word of God.

For example, although the Apostle Paul urged in Ephesians 6:5 that slaves should be obedient to their masters, he was not thereby condoning or approving the practice of slavery. In fact, the principles he laid down in his epistles, especially his letter to Philemon, were of such a nature as to eventually displace this cruel traffic in human beings wherever the gospel took root.

3. *To obtain an over-all view of the spiritual lessons in a book, formulate principles covering basic truths in the main divisions of the book.*

Principles may be derived not only from single verses of Scripture, but also from units of thought such as a paragraph, several successive paragraphs, an entire chapter, or even successive chapters which may be related to one another by a single concept.

For example, a principle derived from Joshua 1 may be stated as follows: The Lord gives divine enablement to the individual He sets in a place of leadership.

We can use the book of Jonah to demonstrate how to derive principles from the main divisions of a book. In the synthetic chart on the book of Jonah which we constructed in chapters 1 and 2, we learned that the book has two main parts. Chapters 1 and 2 relate to Jonah's first commission, and chapters 3 and 4 relate to Jonah's second commission. The principle we formulate will not be simply a repetition of the idea of each main division, but will be a summation of the spiritual truth each main division seems to suggest.

Read through these four chapters of Jonah once more. Then try to think for yourself of a principle which would express the abiding truth each of the main divisions of the book teaches.

Here is the basic truth I see arising out of chapters 1 and 2: We always suffer when we disobey the Lord. I find the following to be the main truth expressed in chapters 3 and 4: God desires the salvation of all men, both Jews and Gentiles.

4. *Enunciate a principle which embodies the main truth of the entire book.*

In previous chapters we have learned that it is not enough to obtain a general view of a book and its relationship to the whole—if we are to understand its message, we must also consider the geographical, cultural, and historical background of the book. Once we have done this, we will be prepared to state the main principle or spiritual lesson of the book.

Earlier chapters have acquainted us with the geographical, cultural, and historical background of Jonah. You recall that Jonah lived in a day of tragic spiritual apostasy in his own land of Israel. The Lord had used various means, including three signs of resurrection, to call His people to repentance. Now, the experience of Jonah, the description of God's chastisement of His disobedient prophet, the turning of the heathen people of Nineveh to God, and the Lord's expression of compassion for the repentant city were all written to call Israel to repentance and to warn God's people of judgment if they continued in their sin.

With all this in mind we propose this theme for the book of Jonah: When men persist in their rejection of God's calls to repentance, they are certain to face judgment. Another way of stating this spiritual truth is as follows: There is no escape from God's judgment for those who stubbornly resist His mercy.

EXERCISE 10

1. Derive two principles for each of the first seven verses of 1 Thessalonians 1.

2. Write a comprehensive principle for each of the two main divisions of 1 Thessalonians. (Chapters 1 through 3 compose the first main division; Chapters 4 and 5 compose the second.)

3. Keeping in mind the basic content of 1 Thessalonians, the geographical, cultural, and historical background of the epistle, and the reasons for its writing, formulate a suitable principle embracing the entire epistle.

4. Prepare a comprehensive principle for each of the four main divisions of the book of Joshua (1-5:12; 5:13-12; 13-22; 23-24).

5. Prepare a comprehensive principle covering the entire book of Joshua in the light of its contents and background.

11. THE TYPOLOGICAL APPROACH

Scriptural Warrant for the Study of Types

There is abundant evidence in the Word of God to indicate that the Lord has designed certain individuals, events, institutions, and objects in the Old Testament to provide us with foregleams or pictures of important truths in the New Testament. When we compare these New Testament truths, or *antitypes*, with their Old Testament foreshadowings, it becomes obvious that the antitypes were actually preordained by God Himself to be the fulfillment of the types which pointed to them or described them in veiled imagery. To ensure that the Scriptures do teach that this is true let us note some specific statements in the New Testament.

Romans 5:14—"Nevertheless, death reigned from the time of Adam to the time of Moses, even over those who did not sin by breaking a command, as did Adam, who was a pattern of the one to come." The term *pattern* in this verse is the Greek word *tupos*, from which we get our English word *type*. We are told specifically in this text that Adam was, in a sense, a type of Christ.

1 Corinthians 10:6—"Now these things occurred as examples, to keep us from setting our hearts on evil things as they did."

1 Corinthians 10:11—"These things happened to them as examples and were written down as warnings for us, on whom the fulfilment of the ages has come."

The word *example* in these references is derived from the identical Greek word *tupos* which appeared in Romans 5:14, meaning type, pattern, or model for imitation or warning.

In these two references in 1 Corinthians 10, the apostle Paul was referring to certain incidents recorded in the Pentateuch, when Israel sinned against the Lord in the wilderness. Paul used these as illustrations to warn believers of the consequences of like disobedience.

Hebrews 8:3-5—"Every high priest is appointed to offer both gifts and sacrifices, and so it was necessary for this one also to have something to offer. If he were on earth, he would not be a priest, for there are already men who offer the gifts prescribed by the law. They serve at a sanctuary that is a copy and shadow of what is in heaven. This is why Moses was warned when he was about to build the tabernacle: 'See to it that you make everything according to the pattern shown you on the mountain.' "

In this passage the word *copy* means an exhibit, figure, or pattern. The term *shadow* connotes an image or outline cast by a shadow, that is, a silhouette or an adumbration.

Hebrews 9:8-9—"The Holy Spirit was showing by this that the way into the Most Holy Place had not yet been disclosed as long as the first tabernacle was still standing. This is an illustration for the present time, indicating that the gifts and sacrifices being offered were not able to clear the conscience of the worshiper."

Here the expression *illustration* comes from the Greek word *parabole*. *Vine's Expository Dictionary of New Testament Words* explains it as something placed side by side with a view to comparison or resemblance. In this passage, the first tabernacle in the wilderness is distinctly stated to be a *parabole* or a purposeful picture of something else with which it should be compared.

Hebrews 10:1—"The law is only a shadow of the good things that are coming—not the realities themselves. For this reason it can never, by the same sacrifices repeated endlessly year after year, make perfect those who draw near to worship."

The expression *shadow* in this verse is precisely the same as in Hebrews 8:5, and suggests a silhouette or an adumbration. This verse thus teaches us that the sacrifices prescribed by the Levitical law were foreshadowings of a better sacrifice yet to come.

Hebrews 11:17-19 (NASB)—"By faith Abraham, when he was tested, offered up Isaac; and he who had received the promises was offering up his only begotten son; it was he to whom it was said, 'In Isaac your descendants shall be called.' He considered that God is able to raise men even from the dead; from which he also received him back as a type."

Here the word *type* is derived from the same Greek word *parabole* as in Hebrews 9:8, and indicates that the return of Isaac was figurative of resurrection.

In addition to these definite and unmistakable statements regarding the presence of types in the Old Testament, there are many other texts in the New Testament which imply that various objects, incidents, persons, or ceremonials in the Old Testament have typical significance. Here are a few of those statements.

John 1:29—"The next day John saw Jesus coming toward him and said, 'Look, the Lamb of God, who takes away the sin of the world!' " We cannot read this text and other similar references to Christ as the Lamb of God without associating them with the story of the passover lamb in Exodus 12.

John 3:14—"Just as Moses lifted up the snake in the desert, so the Son of Man must be lifted up." In this verse the Lord Jesus clearly shows that the serpent of brass, which brought healing to the people of Israel who were bitten by fiery serpents in the wilderness (see Numbers 21:4-9), was a type of Himself.

John 6:30-31—The Jews said to Jesus, "What miraculous sign then will you give that we may see it and believe you? What will you do? Our forefathers ate the manna in the desert; as it is written: 'He gave them bread from heaven to eat.' "

In reply, our Lord delivered His discourse on the bread of life, describing Himself as the bread of life come down from heaven (John 6:32-58). He clearly implied that the manna from heaven which God gave to His people on their journey to Canaan (Exodus 16:4-36) was a foreshadowing of Himself, the Bread of Life.

1 Corinthians 10:4—The Apostle Paul wrote regarding the people of Israel that they ". . . drank the same spiritual drink; for they drank from the spiritual rock that accompanied them, and that rock was Christ." This statement gives incontrovertible proof that the rock smitten by Moses to give water to the people in the desert typified Christ.

Hebrews 6:18-20 (NASB)—". . . we who have fled for refuge in laying hold of the hope set before us. This hope we have as an anchor of the soul, a hope both sure and steadfast and one which enters within the veil, where Jesus has entered as a forerunner for us." We see in these verses a clear reference to the cities of refuge spoken of in Numbers 35:6-34 and other portions of the Old Testament, which portray Christ as a shelter from judgment for the sinner who flees to Him in his need.

Hebrews 10:19-20 (NASB)—"Since therefore, brethren, we have confidence to enter the holy place by the blood of Jesus, by a new and living way which He inaugurated for us through the veil, that is, His flesh." In John 1:14 (NASB) we read, "the Word became flesh, and dwelt among us." And in 1 Timothy 3:16, Paul wrote that God "was revealed in the flesh." Thus, in Hebrews 10:20 the Holy Spirit Himself interprets the veil of the tabernacle as a type of the humanity of the Lord Jesus.

Such an accumulation of evidence in the Scriptures causes us to believe that the resemblances between the types and their antitypes are not accidental. Instead, we are convinced that we have every ground for believing that many portions of the Old Testament were designed by God to carry a likeness to some spiritual truth contained in the New Testament. In the same way, it is no accident that the elements at the Lord's table bear a certain resemblance to the body and blood of Christ, and, in fact, are intended by Him to fit that end. Thus, the correspondence between the types in the Old Testament and the antitypes in the New Testament fulfill the divine purpose of making clearer to us truth as it relates to the Lord Jesus and His word. No other book can claim this; in this respect, Scripture is unique.

Definition of Typology

Typology is the study of certain persons, events, institutions, and objects in the Old Testament that, because of their likeness in various respects to Christ and New Testament truths, enable us to understand and appreciate these truths more fully. In other words, a type is a picture in the Old Testament, in the form of an individual, an event, an institution, a rite, or an object, which God employs to prefigure in an expressive manner some important truth in the New Testament.

Examples of Old Testament Types

In the index at the end of the Scofield Reference Bible there are no less than forty-eight different items listed as types of Christ. Many of these are taken from Chapters 25-40 of Exodus, which describe the tabernacle. Several others are drawn from the book of Leviticus which, almost from beginning to end, contains rites and ceremonies which find their fulfullment in New Testament truth, especially as found in Hebrews 9 and 10.

Lack of space forbids an elaboration of the types in the Old Testament. But we wish to present two examples to show how type and antitype dovetail with one another, leaving no room to doubt that Old Testament types were indeed predesigned by an omniscient Author to give us a foreshadowing of good things to come. So that you may see this for yourself, we suggest that you first read the Scripture passages to which we shall refer.

The Passover

The Passover, described in Exodus 12, is a striking example of a type. Note the following five main features of the Passover lamb, and observe their close resemblance to the Lord Jesus Christ, the antitype.

1. Its divine appointment (Exodus 12:1-3). The lamb was not an idea conceived by Moses or any of the Israelites. It was originated entirely with God. No other plan would have sufficed to deliver the people from the impending judgment in Egypt. It had to be a lamb in accordance with God's express declaration.

When Christ was about to begin His public ministry, John the Baptist declared twice "Behold the Lamb of God" (John 1:29, 36 KJV). Twenty-eight times in the book of Revelation the Apostle John refers to Christ as *the Lamb*. Two other references in the New Testament indicate that this lamb, the Lord Jesus, was specially chosen beforehand as God's instrument for the salvation of mankind.

Note 1 Peter 1:18-20: "For you know that it was not with perishable things such as silver or gold that you were redeemed . . . but with the precious blood of Christ, a lamb without blemish or defect. He was chosen before the creation of the world. . . ." And Revelation 13:8 speaks of "the Lamb that was slain from the creation of the world."

2. Its perfection. Exodus 12:5 states, "The animals you choose must be . . . without defect." Compare this statement with Leviticus 22:21-22 which reads, "When anyone brings from the herd or flock a fellowship offering to the LORD to fulfill a special vow or as a freewill offering it must be without defect or blemish to be acceptable. Do not offer to the LORD the blind, the injured or the maimed, or anything with warts or festering or running sores. Do not place any of these on the altar as an offering made to the LORD by fire."

Thus, the emphasis in the Old Testament was upon a sacrifice which was perfect, for only a perfect sacrifice could meet the demands of a holy God. There is only one individual who could serve as the antitype of the Passover lamb—the perfect Son of God. In Matthew 3:17, the Father said of Jesus, "This is my Son, whom I love; with him I am well pleased." And in Luke 3:22, "You are my Son, whom I love; with you I am well pleased."

3. The manner of its death. Exodus 12:6 declares, ". . . all the people of the community of Israel must slaughter them at twilight." A perfect live lamb could not provide deliverance from the judgment of God in Egypt. Only when it was slain could it become a means of protection. In the same way, though the Lord Jesus Christ, our Passover lamb, lived a perfect life, His sinless life was not the means of our salvation. To become our Savior He had to be put to death. Christ Himself spoke of this before His death when He said, "The Son of Man must suffer many things and be rejected by the elders, chief priests and teachers of the law, and he must be killed" (Luke 9:22).

The following quotations in Revelation 5 lay emphasis upon the same truth. "Then I saw a Lamb, looking as if it had been slain, standing in the center of the throne" (5:6). "And they sang a new song: 'You are worthy to take the scroll and to open its seals, because you were slain, and with your blood you purchased men for God from every tribe and language and people and nation' " (5:9). "In a loud voice they [angels] sang: 'Worthy is the Lamb, who was slain, to receive power and wealth and wisdom and strength and honor and glory and praise!' " (5:12).

Significant also is the instruction given to the people of Israel in Exodus 12:46: "Do not break any of the bones." This is mirrored in Psalm 34:20 in an obvious Messianic reference. It reads, "he protects all his bones, not one of them will be broken." When we examine John 19:32-33 we are told that the soldiers broke the legs of the two men who were crucified with Christ at Calvary, "but when they came to Jesus and found that he was already dead, they did not break his legs." Regarding this, John 19:36 remarks, "These things happened so that the Scripture would be fulfilled: 'Not one of his bones will be broken.' "

4. Its redemptive power. The Passover lamb, after it had been slain, provided protection from judgment to all who applied its blood to the sideposts and the upper door posts of their houses. (See Exodus 12:7, 12-13, 21-23, 28-29.)

And so it is today concerning God's Passover lamb. Because Christ's blood was shed on Calvary's cross in behalf of man's guilt, God has made possible the redemption and deliverance from guilt of every sinner. We read in Galatians 3:13, "Christ redeemed us from the curse of the law by becoming a curse for us, for it is written: 'Cursed is everyone who is hung on a tree.' " In Ephesians 1:7, Paul wrote concerning Christ, "In him we have redemption through his blood, the forgiveness of sins, in accordance with the riches of God's grace." And again Paul wrote in Colossians 1:14 (KJV) "In whom we have redemption through his blood, even the forgiveness of sins."

Observe, however, that even though the Passover lamb had been slain in Egypt, its blood had to be applied by each household if the people of Israel were to be spared from the judgment which was about to fall upon Egypt. In the same way, although Christ our Passover lamb died upon the cross for the redemption of mankind, His blood must be applied by each guilty individual who is under God's just sentence of spiritual death, if he is to escape God's wrath against sin. That application is made by faith. This means that each one of us must wholly put his trust in what Christ has done on the cross if he is to be saved from sin. Note John 3:36: "Whoever believes in the Son has eternal life, but whoever rejects the Son will not see life, for God's wrath remains on him."

5. Its sustaining power. The same lamb which was slain to provide protection for the people of Israel also became their sustenance as they started out from Egypt on their pilgrimage to Canaan. Feeding upon the Passover lamb gave them strength for the long journey which lay before them (Exodus 12:8-11, 43-50).

In the same way, Christ, who gave His life for us to redeem us from sin, also gives His life to us. He said, "The one who feeds on me will live because of me" (John 6:57). In other words, we must feed upon Christ, our life, to be sustained during our pilgrimage upon this earth.

Manna

A second example of a type is the manna, recorded in Exodus 16:4-36, which fed the pilgrims during their journey in the wilderness. It is a picture of the spiritual food upon which the Lord's people should feed during their pilgrimage on this earth. Let us note five main facts about manna to see how it resembles the spiritual food of the believer today.

1. The source of the manna. Exodus 16:4 quotes a statement made by the Lord to Moses: "I will rain down bread from heaven for you." In verse 15 of the same chapter, after the manna had come down upon the earth, Moses declared to the people, "It is the bread the LORD has

given you to eat."

Referring to the same incident, the Psalmist wrote, "He gave a command to the skies above and opened the doors of the heavens; he rained down manna for the people to eat, he gave them the grain of heaven. Men ate the bread of angels" (Psalm 78:23-25).

In His great discourse on the Bread of Life in John 6:22-58, the Lord Jesus declared four times that he was the Bread of Life which came down from heaven (verses 33, 38, 50, 51). Christ can be to us today all that the manna was to Israel—and more. Feeding on Him through His Word, we are filled with bread from heaven. The manna fed only the bodies of the Israelites; Christ feeds our souls. The manna satisfied only physical hunger; Christ satisfies our spiritual hunger. The manna kept only the bodies of the people alive in the wilderness; Christ gives us eternal life in Himself.

2. The supernatural character of the manna. Some have claimed that the provision of the manna was no miracle at all, asserting that it was found on certain trees in the area, such as the prickly *alhagi* (sometimes called the "Sinai manna") or the *tamarisk,* which exude a gum resin. But the manna which came down upon the camp of the Israelites had certain distinctives which were unquestionably miraculous. It fell regularly on six days of the week, but never on the seventh; it could never be kept fresh from one day to the next, except on the sixth day, when it remained fresh through the seventh day, the Hebrews' day of rest; and it provided amply for a vast company of people (perhaps as many as two million) in the wilderness—not for a day or a week or even a whole month, but for forty years. The manna did not cease until the day after the Israelites first ate of the food of the land of Canaan (Joshua 5:11-12), when they no longer had to rely on the provision of manna to survive. With this evidence, who can doubt the miraculous nature of the manna?

And the spiritual provision which the Lord makes for His people on their earthly pilgrimage is no less miraculous. Like the manna, Christ is the spiritual food upon which His people must feed. And the birth, life, death, and resurrection of Jesus Christ were all of a supernatural character. Matthew quotes the prophecy of Isaiah, written hundreds of years before Christ's birth: " 'The virgin will be with child and will give birth to a son, and they will call him Immanuel'—which means, 'God with us' " (Matthew 1:23).

In the same way, the Bible, the written Word which reveals the Living Word, is also miraculous both in its origin and in its effects upon men. Note the following Scriptures: 2 Timothy 3:16-17—"All Scripture is God-breathed and is useful for teaching, rebuking, correcting and training in righteousness, so that the man of God may be thoroughly equipped for every good work"; Hebrews 4:12—"The word of God is living and active. Sharper than any double-edged sword, it penetrates even to dividing soul and spirit, joints and marrow; it judges the thoughts and attitudes of the heart"; and in John 6:63 the Lord Jesus said, "The words I have spoken to you are spirit and they are life."

3. The taste of the manna. Exodus 16:31 states that it "tasted like wafers made with honey." It was sweet. This reminds us of the Psalmist's description of the Word of God as being "sweeter than honey . . . from the comb" (Psalm 19:10).

Many years later the prophet Jeremiah wrote, "Thy words were found, and I did eat them; and thy word was unto me the joy and rejoicing of mine heart" (Jeremiah 15:16 KJV).

4. The collecting of the manna. Note these four facts in relation to the collecting of the manna. It had to be gathered by every man (vv. 16, 18, 21). It had to be gathered fresh every day (v. 4). It had to be gathered early every day (v. 21). It had to be gathered according to every man's need (vv. 17, 18, 21).

These instructions correspond closely to the way in which the believer is to feed upon the Scriptures for himself. The Lord Jesus said, "Man does not live on bread alone, but on every word that comes from the mouth of God" (Matthew 4:4). And of the fruitful believer, He said, "If you remain in me and my words remain in you, ask whatever you wish, and it will be given you" (John 15:7). Again, Jesus said, "Whoever eats my flesh and drinks my blood remains in me, and I in him" (John 6:56).

5. The purpose of the manna. Exodus 16:35 says that "the Israelites ate manna forty years, until they came to the land that was settled; they ate manna until they reached the borders of Canaan." In other words, manna was the divine provision for the Israelites throughout their pilgrimage in the wilderness; apart from the quail which the Lord brought them once, manna was their only food. So it is with the Bible. God has given it to us as our one and only form of spiritual sustenance during our pilgrimage on this earth. In 2 Timothy 3:16, 17, Paul wrote, "All Scripture is God-breathed and is useful for teaching, re-

buking, correcting and training in righteousness, so that the man of God may be thoroughly equipped for every good work."

But there came a time when the people of Israel despised their heavenly food. We read in Numbers 21:5 that the people "spoke against God and against Moses, and said, 'Why have you brought us up out of Egypt to die in the desert? There is no bread! There is no water! And we detest this miserable food!' " Because of their wicked rejection of God's heavenly provision, the Lord sent poisonous snakes among the people, resulting in many deaths. It is possible for the Christian, too, to despise God's Holy Word, to neglect reading it and feeding on the living bread. But if he does, he can be sure that poisonous snakes will come, too, in the form of sin of one kind or another with its terrible sting of anguish, loss, regret, and remorse. How well for us to remember what someone once said: "Sin will keep you from this book or this book will keep you from sin."

In our two examples of types—the Passover and the manna—we have touched only upon the more significant parallels between type and antitype. But we believe that these two examples are sufficient to prove that the likenesses between type and antitype are not accidental, but are recorded for our instruction in and deeper appreciation of the person and work of Christ, and our relationship to His Word.

Principles for the Study of Types

1. Consider something as a type only when there is definite New Testament authentication for it.

Because there are so many clearly defined statements in the New Testament regarding the presence of Old Testament types, some have gone to the extreme of seeking typical or figurative meaning in almost everything in the Scriptures, even to the most minute details, giving an allegorical or fanciful interpretation to much of the Bible. This was the error of the early church fathers. To them practically everything in the Scriptures had a deeper, hidden spiritual meaning other than the obvious literal meaning of the text.

For example, Clement of Alexandria, who lived at the end of the second century A.D., thought that the best robe the father gave to the prodigal son upon his return home represented immortality, the shoes spoke of the upward trend of the soul, and the fatted calf was a symbol of Christ, the spiritual sustenance of those who partake of Him.

Some modern interpreters of the Scriptures are no less extreme. Joshua 15:8 (KJV), describing the border of the territory of the tribe of Judah, reads in part, "the border went up to the top of the mountain that lieth before the valley of Hinnom westward, which is at the end of the valley of the giants northward." One writer explains that the giants are a type of the enemies' power. They may be considered superhuman and can overthrow by sight any individual who merely looks at them. The top of the mountain speaks of separation. It is a judgment of sin rather than the effect of the superhuman power of the enemy.

In the same vein, another writer interprets one edge of the two-edged sword mentioned in Hebrews 4:12 and Revelation 1:16 as the Old Testament, and the other edge as the New Testament.

However, in the case of Jonah we have ample evidence that he was meant to be a type of New Testament truth, for he is the one and only individual in the Old Testament with whom the Lord Jesus compared Himself. In fact, when we note what Christ said in Matthew 12:38-41, Matthew 16:4, and Luke 11:29-32, it is clear that Christ regarded Jonah's experience and ministry as being of special typical significance.

We would make just one exception to this rule. Although Joseph is never referred to in the New Testament as a type of Christ, the parallels between the Old Testament patriarch and the Lord Jesus are so extraordinary that we are forced to conclude that he was divinely intended to be a special foreshadowing of our Savior.

2. Look up every reference in the Scriptures to the type, if possible.

When the type is described in the Bible by a single word or phrase, you will find an unabridged concordance to be helpful in locating its various occurrences. If, however, the type is described in Scripture under more than one name, a Bible dictionary or Bible encyclopedia may help you discover the other names used and all their locations. Noting every occurrence in the Bible of the type enables us to obtain a complete picture of the type.

3. Make sure there is obvious resemblance or congruity between the type and the antitype.

Since, as we have seen, types fall into various categories, such as persons, events, institutions or rites, and objects, the similarities will necessarily vary with the nature of the type. Furthermore, the resemblances between type and antitype in one case will differ beween type and antitype in another case depending on the purpose the Holy Spirit had in mind when they were recorded.

This is the principle the apostles used to adduce the likeness that existed between the type and the person or thing it typified. For example, note the correspondence between the burnt offering described in Leviticus 1:1-9, and Paul's statement in Ephesians 5:2 that Christ "gave himself up for us as a fragrant offering and sacrifice to God."

Like the Passover lamb, the burnt offering had to be without blemish, just as Christ was sinless and without fault. But the distinctive feature of the burnt offering was that it was wholly given to God as a sacrifice. It speaks of Christ's complete devotion to doing the will of God by sacrificing Himself on the cross. In both instances the sacrifice was a sweet smelling savour to God (Psalm 40:5-8; Hebrews 10:5-17). The Old Testament worshiper's acceptance before God was based not upon his own merits but entirely upon the acceptability of his offering. In the case of the believer today, his acceptance is dependent wholly upon the perfection of Jesus Christ, his slain lamb.

With respect to Joseph, the resemblance between his life and that of Christ is particularly striking. Note, for instance, the main features of Joseph's life in relation to his brothers, as recorded in Genesis. In chapters 37-40 we see his rejection by his brothers, in chapters 41-44 his exaltation apart from his brothers, and in chapters 45-50 his manifestation to his brothers. No devout student of the Word of God can fail to see in this biographical outline a remarkable adumbration of the Lord Jesus in relation to His people, Israel.

Again, the life of Joseph may be seen in regard to three other successive emphases: He was first a son, then a sufferer, and then a ruler. Once more Christ's life is here foreseen as He, the "rejected brother," takes His place in glory as ruler following His suffering (Luke 24:16; 1 Peter 1:11). A careful examination of the record of Joseph's life will reveal many more likenesses between him and our blessed Savior. But we shall leave it to the reader to pursue this profitable study for himself.

When we come to the book of Jonah we observe that the length of Christ's burial was identical with that of Jonah's entombment in the fish. This striking resemblance between Christ and Jonah in this one respect leads us to believe that there must be other important parallels between Jonah as a type and the Lord Jesus as the antitype. We therefore dig deeper into the book of Jonah and compare his life with that of Christ to discover other areas of resemblance.

First of all, note that both Jonah and the Lord Jesus were prophets. It is also interesting to observe that both came from Galilee. Unfortunately, Jonah proved to be a recalcitrant prophet, whereas the Lord Jesus was a prophet who honored God in all His ways.

Jonah was given a unique commission from God; so was his divine successor.

Then, Jonah's entombment in the fish prefigured the death and burial of Christ. It is interesting to observe that Jonah's prayer from the belly of the fish consisted of numerous quotations from the Psalms. In fact, his prayer may be said to be a medley of Psalms. And in Luke 24:44, the Lord Jesus Himself said, "This is what I told you while I was still with you: Everything must be fulfilled that is written about me in the Law of Moses, the Prophets and the Psalms." This has led some Bible scholars to conclude that Jonah's prayer (Jonah 2) is Messianic and to a large degree expressive of the agonies which Christ endured in His passion.

Another area of resemblance between Jonah and Christ is the restoration of Jonah to life, in a manner of speaking, following his entombment for three days and three nights. This is a type of Christ's resurrection from the dead, as the Lord Himself has made abundantly clear. (See Matthew 12:38-41; 16:4; and Luke 11:29-32.)

Finally, just as Jonah's apparent restoration to life following his entombment became a sign to the people of Nineveh, so the actual resurrection of Christ from the dead became a sign to the people of His day, and to mankind ever since. Thus, Jonah's narrative is, by its very typical character, a prophetic picture of One greater than Jonah.

4. Discover the main resemblances between the type and its antitype.

Obviously, the type and antitype can never be identical; the former is intended only to be a foregleam or foreshadowing of the latter. Thus we must not attempt to find identification in all respects between the type and its antitype. Rather, we should seek the important features in the two which are analogous with each other. At the same time, to prove the legitimacy of each analogy, we should have sound Scriptural support for each premise; otherwise we may be in danger of spiritualizing the text or making interpretations which are the product of fantasy.

5. Do not attempt to establish a doctrine upon a type.

As we have seen, types are shadows, and a shadow implies substance. The substance is found in the antitype. The type is given to us, therefore, to illustrate or to draw our attention emphatically and vividly to the antitype. This being the case, we must avoid basing any doctrine upon a type. For instance, as we have just learned, the doctrine of the resurrection of Christ is not based upon the narrative of Jonah but upon the fact of Christ's actual resurrection as recorded in the gospels and explained in the epistles.

6. Seek the outstanding practical truth which the study of the type suggests.

There are many practical truths which can be drawn from the consideration of a type, and, as always, we need the Spirit of God to show us what He wants us to learn from this kind of Bible study. But as we study the type and its antitype, one outstanding spiritual lesson should emerge. In Jonah, the outstanding feature is clearly the idea of resurrection. And in the light of New Testament doctrine about the resurrection of Jesus Christ we see this glorious and practical truth: Because of Christ's resurrection, the believer is united with Him in His victory over every evil thing.

I came to know Christ as my personal Savior when I was a boy of thirteen. When I grew to be a young man, doubts began to creep into my mind whether the Bible was really the Word of God. I decided that the best way for me to settle the question was to enroll as a student at Moody Bible Institute. I expected the professors there to give me specific answers to my questions and to prove to me that the Scriptures were indeed inspired of God.

However, in my first semester at Moody I was given an assignment for a class in Bible synthesis to read the Bible for two and one half hours every week, beginning with Genesis. When I reached Exodus, chapter 12, the Holy Spirit showed me that here, in the account of the Passover, was a perfect foreshadowing of Jesus Christ, the Lamb of God. When I saw the picture of God's sinless lamb depicted so clearly in the book of Exodus, I realized that no human mind could have drawn such a perfect analogy—so many hundreds of years before Christ came into the world—between the Passover lamb and the Lord Jesus Christ. God, by His Holy Spirit, opened my eyes at that moment to behold the Lamb of God who takes away the sin of the world. Seeing Him, my every doubt vanished forever.

"Therefore, since we have so great a cloud of witnesses surrounding us, let us also lay aside every encumbrance, and the sin which so easily entangles us, and let us run with endurance the race that is set before us, fixing our eyes on Jesus" (Hebrews 12:1, 2 NASB).

EXERCISE 11

1. Read Numbers 21:4-9 and John 3:14-15 carefully and with prayer. Then, with the knowledge you have gained in this chapter on the study of typology, try to discover in what respects the bronze snake which Moses set up in the wilderness was a type of the Lord Jesus. Give adequate explanation of each item and support each premise with Scriptural proof. Avoid the use of any outside helps except a concordance and a Bible dictionary or Bible encyclopedia.

2. What outstanding principle or truth can you draw from the study of the bronze snake as a type of Christ?

Answers to Exercises

EXERCISE 1

The Purpose of Your Synthetic Study

Since this may have been your very first attempt at constructing a synthetic chart, you may feel that your chart leaves much to be desired. Nevertheless, because it is your very own work, done without the aid of any book other than your own Bible, you now have a much better knowledge of 1 Thessalonians than you have ever had before. You can think through the epistle beginning with Paul's salutation and thanks for the young church in Thessalonica and you can trace in your own mind all the important developments right through to its conclusion and benediction.

Having completed your own chart of 1 Thessalonians, you can now examine mine and follow my outline with ease. Open your Bible now to 1 Thessalonians. Note the words in each diagonal space in the chart and compare them with the Scripture portion referred to by the chart. Observe that these sections contain a summary of each paragraph in the epistle. These paragraph summaries are vital to our grasp of the contents of the book.

A Brief Summary of 1 Thessalonians

Looking at the paragraph summaries, observe the relationship of paragraphs two through seven. Each one of them deals in some way with Paul's personal relationship with the Thessalonians. Hence, we have grouped these paragraphs to form the first main division of the epistle. Then the emphasis shifts at 4:1; Paul concentrates on exhortation and instruction. The paragraph which begins at 5:23 and concludes at 5:24 is a prayer which climaxes the teaching he has just given them concerning Christian life and conduct. We have therefore combined these paragraphs to form our second main division. Both Jonah and 1 Thessalonians have just two main divisions. This is not true of every book in the Bible. Some have three main divisions, others four, and some as many as five or six, depending upon the contents of the book.

Because Jonah and this book are brief, we have summarized their contents by paragraphs instead of by chapters. The very same principles for the construction of a synthetic chart apply to an extended book as they do to a book of only a few chapters. We simply summarize the contents chapter by chapter in the case of a longer book. You will find in chapter 7 the chart of a book with many more chapters than those we have considered thus far.

Making Your Study Personal

Do not be discouraged if your work on 1 Thessalonians does not approximate mine. Nothing can substitute for your very own study under the guidance of the Holy Spirit. We are not opposed to the use of other helps; you shouldn't disregard the spiritual insight which the Lord has given to His people who have diligently pondered over His Word in the past. But your own study must be done first without the aid of others if you are to learn how to study a book in the Bible yourself.

Did you see anything of special significance as you read through the epistle of 1 Thessalonians and summarized the book paragraph by paragraph? We won't take the time as we did in Jonah to go through the book paragraph by paragraph, but let's stop and look at one significant item under the very first paragraph in 1 Thessalonians.

We read in chapter 1:1 that Paul mentions a team of co-workers in his address to the church. He begins his epistle by saying, "Paul and Silvanus (or Silas) and Timothy to the church of the Thessalonians" and so on. The very fact that Paul refers specifically to Silas and Timothy together with himself in connection with his ministry in Thessalonica suggests to us that as Paul carried out his missionary service, he did not labor alone but he worked together with others. And it indicates to us that God's work is often done best when His people work together as one.

There are many other vital facts to be observed and vital truths to be drawn from this epistle, and we suggest that you keep a looseleaf notebook to record any thoughts that come to your mind as you study further.

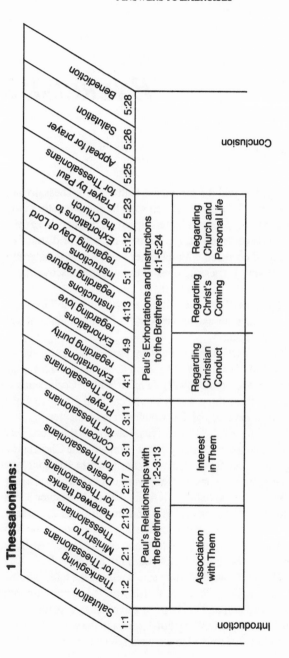

Figure 14

EXERCISE 2

You were asked to find the prominent features in 1 Thessalonians and to classify them. That is to say, you were to group together those items which seem to bear some relationship to one another. In keeping with the other parts of the chart, the items in each set of distinctives were to be balanced or mated with the other items in the same group.

Let us now review 1 Thessalonians with a view to discovering its important features.

Beginning at chapter 1, our attention is arrested in verse 3 by an unusual combination of phrases. "Your work of faith and labor of love and steadfastness of hope."

As we look more carefully at these three phrases we note a significant word at the end of each one. The word *faith*, the word *love*, and the word *hope*. You are undoubtedly familiar with 1 Corinthians 13 and will recall that these three words are the cardinal graces to which the apostle refers at the close of that wonderful love chapter.

Continued reading of 1 Thessalonians uncovers the word *faith* again in verse 8 of chapter 1, used in connection with the Christians at Thessalonica. Then, in chapter 2, Paul writes in verse 10 about "you believers." And again in verse 13 of the "word of God, which also performs its work in you who believe (NASB)." Then in chapter 3 Paul speaks five times of "your faith." We find this in verse 2, verse 5, verse 6, verse 7, and verse 10. It is interesting that although the KJV renders the words in verse 6 as "your faith and charity," the NASB and the NIV maintain our beautiful duet: "your faith and love."

Moving to chapter 5, we find that verse 8 tells of the three cardinal graces again. Paul writes, "let us be self-controlled, putting on faith and love as a breastplate, and the hope of salvation as a helmet." Observe that Paul gives these three cardinal graces in the same order here as he gave them in 1:3. From what we have seen so far, we may conclude that these three graces are among the special emphases of this epistle.

At this point we should retrace our steps and read through the epistle once more. Repeated readings are not wasting time, for the more we read the Scriptures in a prayerful, reverent spirit, the more we will learn from the Word of God and the greater our blessing will be.

Our second reading of the epistle impresses us with Paul's love for the believers of this church which he had founded. Although (except for 1:3) Paul does not use the word "love" at all in chapters 1 and 2, these two chapters seem to breathe a spirit of deep affection for these young Christians who were his very own spiritual children.

Read especially 2:7-11. These verses hold such phrases as, "like a mother caring for her little children," "we loved you so much," "you had become so dear to us," and "as a father deals with his own children."

Then in 2:17-3:10 Paul writes of his intense longing to come to the Thessalonian believers once again, a longing which, he tells them, causes him to pray night and day that he might see them again. Paul has such great love for these saints that he addresses them throughout the epistle by the affectionate term, "brethren."

Our reading of this epistle makes it apparent that Paul's love for the brethren of Thessalonica was real, intense, and sacrificial. But the apostle also refers to the fervent love that the Thessalonian brethren had for him and his co-workers. "But Timothy has just now come to us from you and has brought good news about your faith and love. He has told us that you always have pleasant memories of us and that you long to see us, just as we also long to see you" (3:6).

Although Paul was comforted and encouraged by the reciprocal affection of the Thessalonian converts, he also wanted the brethren to have the same affection for each other as they had for him. This is evident in his prayer in chapter 3: "Now may our God and Father himself and our Lord Jesus clear the way for us to come to you. May the Lord make your love increase and overflow for each other and for everyone else, just as ours does for you" (3:11-12).

In chapter 4, Paul again exhorts the Thessalonian brethren: "Now about brotherly love we do not need to write to you, for you yourselves have been taught by God to love each other. And in fact, you do love all the brothers throughout Macedonia. Yet we urge you, brothers, to do so more and more" (4:9-10).

Paul's repeated references to love—Paul's love for the Thessalo-

nian believers, their love for Paul, and their love for one another—
make it evident that, like faith, love is another major emphasis of this
epistle.

The third cardinal grace, hope, is also a major emphasis of 1 Thessalonians.

In 1:9-10 Paul writes, "for they themselves report what kind of reception you gave us. They tell how you turned to God from idols to
serve the living and true God, and to wait for his Son from heaven,
whom he raised from the dead—Jesus, who rescues us from the coming wrath."

Thus Paul first mentions the believer's hope in the coming of the
Lord Jesus at the climax of chapter 1. He brings up the subject again at
the close of chapter 2. There we read, "For what is our hope, our joy,
or the crown in which we will glory in the presence of our Lord Jesus
when He comes? Is it not you?" (2:19)

And Paul writes about it again at the end of chapter 3. "May he
strengthen your hearts so that you will be blameless and holy in the
presence of our God and Father when our Lord Jesus comes with all his
holy ones" (3:13).

Then in chapter 4 Paul devotes an entire section at the end of the
chapter to the subject of the Lord's return (4:13-18). He continues his
discussion of the coming of the Lord in chapter 5. As he concludes his
epistle, Paul makes one last reference (5:23) to the second coming of
the Lord Jesus Christ. There we read, "May God himself, the God of
peace, sanctify you through and through. May your whole spirit, soul
and body be kept blameless at the coming of our Lord Jesus Christ."

Thus each chapter in this epistle ends with a specific reference to
the coming of Christ. Furthermore, this small book of only five chapters devotes a great deal of space in chapters 4 and 5 to the second coming of Christ. These things make it clear to us that, like the other two
cardinal graces, hope is also a major emphasis of 1 Thessalonians.

One more look at the epistle of 1 Thessalonians reveals another aspect of the three cardinal graces. In chapter 1, Paul refers to the faith
which the believers had exercised in the past in the gospel message. In
the second and third chapters and the first part of the fourth chapter,
Paul speaks in the present tense of the love he has for the believers, and
of their love for him and for each other. Then Paul directs the believers' attention to their future hope in the second coming of Christ.
Thus, we associate these cardinal graces with the three tenses of the
Christian life: the past, the present, and the future.

We have now completed one group of concepts in the epistle, the
cardinal graces of the Christian life, and are ready for a second group.
Even a cursory examination of 1 Thessalonians will indicate that a

large portion of the epistle deals with Paul's ministry to the believers in Thessalonica. But a close scrutiny will reveal certain characteristics of this ministry which the Holy Spirit recorded for our benefit. Observe the following qualities of Paul's ministry.

First, it was a prayerful ministry (1:2, 3; 3:9, 10; 3:11-13; 5:23).

Next, it was a ministry characterized by love (1:3; 2:7-11; 3:6, 11-12; 4:9-10).

Third, it was an exemplary ministry (2:9-12).

Fourth, it was a ministry of comfort (3:1-4; 4:13-18; 5:1-11).

Finally, it was an intensely practical ministry (4:1-10; 5:12-22). In these verses, Paul presents many practical matters relating to the life and conduct of the believer.

There are several other characteristics of Paul's ministry to be found in these chapters, but the five we have listed are the most significant. We may now add these main features of 1 Thessalonians to our chart. This enables us to see in the chart the entire epistle at a glance. The diagonal sections show our summary of each paragraph. We have grouped these summaries together to form the main divisions of the book, and then we have broken up these main divisions once more to see more clearly the structure of the book.

With the prominent features placed under the synthetic chart, we get a comprehensive view of the whole. Note that we have grouped the distinctives of the book together with the cardinal graces of the Christian life in one section, and below that the characteristics of Paul's ministry. Also observe that all the main emphases are expressed succinctly and are balanced or mated together with the other items in each group.

To finish the chart we add a title which we place directly under the name of the book: "Paul's First Letter of Encouragement to the Believers in Thessalonica." We have chosen this title because of the references in the epistle to the suffering and sorrow of the believers and the way Paul encouraged them in their distress, particularly by his great emphasis on their future hope.

We are sure that as a result of your own study of 1 Thessalonians you will have observed at least one or two of the items we have shown to be major emphases of the book. Even if you did not, however, your own independent study of this portion of God's Word will have given you a deeper knowledge of 1 Thessalonians than you ever had before.

But unless we apply what we have learned from our study, we have merely a group of facts which are of no practical value to us. We might apply one of the distinctives we found in 1 Thessalonians by considering it in the following fashion.

This is probably the first letter that Paul ever wrote to a church. And he places special emphasis on the love that believers should have for one another. But, he says, this love should not just be talked about—it should be put into practice. If I call myself a Christian, I, too, must love my fellow believers, for I can teach others to love only as I exemplify love in my own life and relationships with other Christians.

Consider in what ways you might apply the other distinctives we discovered in 1 Thessalonians to your life. And as you meditate on these things and lay yourself open to the Spirit of God, He will reveal what you need to know and give you grace to become conformed to the image of Jesus Christ.

1 Thessalonians: Paul's First Letter of Encouragement to the Believers at Thessalonica

Salutation 1:1	Thanksgiving for Thessalonians 1:2	Ministry to Thessalonians 2:1	Renewed thanks for Thessalonians 2:13	Desire for Thessalonians 2:17	Concern for Thessalonians 3:1	Prayer for Thessalonians 3:11	Exhortations regarding purity 4:1	Exhortations regarding love 4:9	Instructions regarding rapture 4:13	Instructions regarding Day of Lord 5:1	Exhortations to the Church 5:12	Prayer by Paul for Thessalonians 5:23	Appeal for prayer 5:25	Salutation 5:26	Benediction 5:28

Introduction	Paul's Relationships with the Brethren 1:2–3:13		Paul's Exhortations and Instructions to the Brethren 4:1–5:24			Conclusion
	Association with Them	Interest in Them	Regarding Christian Conduct	Regarding Christ's Coming	Regarding Church and Personal Life	
	The Past	The Present		The Future		
	Faith in God	Love for the Brethren		Hope in Christ		
		Paul's Ministry				
	Prayerful Loving Exemplary Comforting Practical					

Figure 15

EXERCISE 3

We asked you to apply the rules given in chapter 3 to discover all the geographical information you could which pertains to 1 Thessalonians. The process is so obvious that we will not go through the steps we took or list the sources we used.

After comparing the places Paul mentions in 1 Thessalonians with the record in Acts 17:1-18:11 concerning the founding of the church at Thessalonica and what followed, we drew a rough map showing the route Paul took through Macedonia and Achaia during his second missionary journey. We have listed below the map a series of events leading up to the writing of 1 Thessalonians. (See Figure 16.)

We are sure that you will have come to the same conclusions as we have in our geographical study of 1 Thessalonians; that is, that one of Paul's primary purposes in writing this letter was to comfort God's people in that young church who so early in their existence were going through persecution and trial. Isn't this always God's way with His own? He permits His beloved children to suffer but he "comforts us in all our troubles, so that we can comfort those in any trouble with the comfort we ourselves have received from God" (2 Corinthians 1:4).

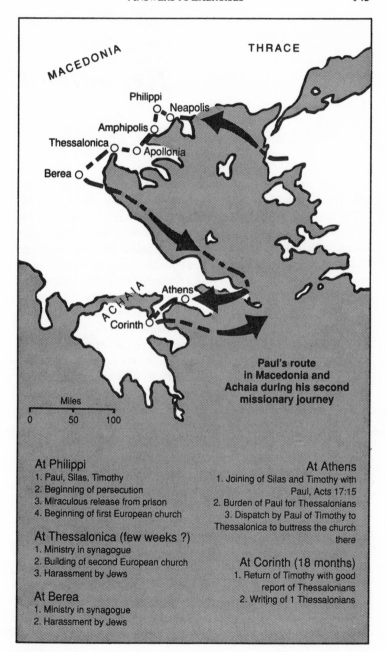

Paul's route
in Macedonia and
Achaia during his second
missionary journey

At Philippi
1. Paul, Silas, Timothy
2. Beginning of persecution
3. Miraculous release from prison
4. Beginning of first European church

At Thessalonica (few weeks ?)
1. Ministry in synagogue
2. Building of second European church
3. Harassment by Jews

At Berea
1. Ministry in synagogue
2. Harassment by Jews

At Athens
1. Joining of Silas and Timothy with
Paul, Acts 17:15
2. Burden of Paul for Thessalonians
3. Dispatch by Paul of Timothy to
Thessalonica to buttress the church
there

At Corinth (18 months)
1. Return of Timothy with good
report of Thessalonians
2. Writing of 1 Thessalonians

Figure 16

EXERCISE 4

1. One can glean many cultural features from a study of 1 Thessalonians. For example, Christians associated together in an assembly called the church. The members of the church were governed by leaders who were to be respected. The Thessalonian Christians had a close spiritual relationship with one another and called each other brethren; that is, members together of a spiritual family. Some of them had once worshiped idols, but now they all worshiped God. They were joyful believers in spite of having suffered much persecution. They loved one another, and they loved their spiritual father, the Apostle Paul. They were also active in spreading the Word of God.

2. Different groups originally composed the church at Thessalonica, as indicated in Acts 17:1-11. Some were Jews who had heard Paul preaching in the synagogue. Others were Gentiles, Greeks who feared God. A number of the prominent women of the city were members of the Thessalonian church.

3. There are many cultural patterns which shed light on ancient Thessalonica. Here are five.

a. While most of the people were Macedonians, there was also a Jewish settlement in the city.

b. Thessalonica was under the control of Rome, which had appointed a board of five politarchs, or magistrates, to govern the city.

c. The location of Thessalonica along the Egnatian Way, which the Romans had built to facilitate the movement of troops across Macedonia, made it a place of considerable commerce.

d. Latin was the official language of the Romans, but Greek was commonly spoken by the citizens of Thessalonica. No doubt many of the Jews in Thessalonica were able to speak both Greek and Hebrew or Aramaic.

e. The moral level of the city of Thessalonica was extremely low;

146

temple "virgins" were used in many pagan religious rites all over the Roman world.

EXERCISE 5

1. Pertinent information about the author of 1 Thessalonians.

a. Proof of Paul's authorship.

Internal evidence shows that Paul was the author (1 Thessalonians 1:1, 2:18). Comparison of historical references to Paul in the book of Acts and the epistles agree (compare 1 Thessalonians 2:2 with Acts 16:22, 23; 1 Thessalonians 2:17 with Acts 18:5; 1 Thessalonians 3:4 with Acts 17:5).

b. Brief history of Paul's training and ministry.

He was born of Hebrew parents and trained in accordance with the best traditions of Judaism. At the same time he was a citizen of Tarsus and of the Roman Empire. He grew up in a Hellenistic culture and was endowed with a great intellect. He was thus ideally suited as God's chosen vessel to reach both Jew and Gentile with the Gospel and to teach the churches which he founded during his missionary journeys. Together with Silas and Timothy, Paul established the church in Thessalonica on his second missionary journey.

2. Time and place of the writing of the epistle.

Scholars generally agree that it was written about A.D. 50 or 51. This would make it the first letter we have on record by the Apostle.

Scripture would indicate that the epistle was written shortly after the founding of the church at Thessalonica. Silas and Timothy visited Paul at Athens (Acts 17:15). Paul then sent Timothy back to Thessalonica to encourage the new converts (1 Thessalonians 3:1-3). Both Silas and Timothy then returned to Paul at Corinth with the report about the church (Acts 18:5). Timothy's report prompted Paul to write the letter from Corinth.

3. Significant facts about the recipients.

Some of the new converts were Jews, but among the Gentiles were a few prominent women of the city as well as many people who had once been heathen idol worshipers. Having come to know the Lord through Paul's ministry, they had become ardent Christians with a warmth of Christian love among themselves and a zeal to spread the good news of salvation far and wide in spite of persecution.

However, the believers had misunderstood Paul's teaching about the Lord's return (1 Thessalonians 4:13-18). Some had given up their jobs thinking that the Lord's coming was imminent (1 Thessalonians 2:9; 4:11). Some were apparently misusing their spiritual gifts (1 Thessalonians 5:19-21). And evidently some of the Gentile converts were being tempted to return to former sexual impurities (1 Thessalonians 4:1-8). But the converts were loyal to Paul and were looking forward to his return to them (1 Thessalonians 3:1-8).

4. Reasons for the writing of the epistle.

There were many reasons why Paul wrote to the young Thessalonian church. He wanted to express his personal interest in them and thus to strengthen the bonds between himself and them. He also wanted to commend the believers for their faith (1 Thessalonians 1:3), to exhort them to moral purity (1 Thessalonians 4:1-8), to correct erroneous views about the return of the Lord Jesus Christ (1 Thessalonians 4:13-18), and to encourage them as they were facing persecution (1 Thessalonians 2:13-16).

EXERCISE 6

Having read 1 Thessalonians and noted all significant biographical facts, we have organized these facts below to show ten character traits of the Apostle Paul.

1. He was cooperative.
   He worked together with Silas and Timothy, 1:1.
2. He was grateful.
   (1) He gave thanks to God for the vital Christian life of the Thessalonian believers, 1:3.
   (2) He gave thanks to God for the Thessalonians' reception of the Word, 2:13.
   (3) He desired to give more thanks to God because of his joy over the Thessalonians, 3:9.
3. He was loving.
   (1) He regarded the Thessalonian believers as his brothers, and emphasized this by repeatedly calling them "brothers," 1:4; 2:1, 9, 14, 17; 3:7; 4:1, 10, 13; 5:1, 4, 12, 14, 25, 26, 27.
   (2) He was willing to give his own life to minister to the Thessalonian believers, 2:8.
   (3) He toiled night and day to refrain from burdening the new believers financially with his upkeep, 2:9.
   (4) He dealt with the new believers as a father deals with his own children, 2:11.
   (5) He longed to be with the believers after his forcible separation from them, and he repeatedly attempted to return to them, 2:17.
   (6) He was willing to be left alone in Athens when he sent Timothy to minister to the spiritual needs of the new

believers, 3:1-2.

(7) He found joy in learning from Timothy of the steadfast-ness of the believers in their faith and love, 3:6-7.

4. He was courageous.

He dared to proclaim the Gospel to the Thessalonians in spite of danger and opposition, 2:2.

5. He was faithful.

(1) He proclaimed the Gospel as one to whom a sacred trust had been committed, 2:4.

(2) He taught the new believers what they needed to know about living to please God, 4:1-12.

(3) He instructed them about the coming of the Lord for His own and about the Day of the Lord, 4:13-5:11.

(4) He exhorted them and instructed them about their rela-tionship with the elders of the church, among them-selves, and to the Lord, 5:12-21.

6. He was sincere.

He ministered the Word of God from pure motives, as approved by God, 2:4.

7. He was gentle.

He treated the Thessalonian believers like a nursing mother in her care for her child, 2:7.

8. He was upright.

He lived a holy and blameless life before God and before the Thessalonian believers, 2:10.

9. He was sympathetic.

(1) He sought to comfort the Thessalonians in their persecu-tions, 3:2-4.

(2) He sought to comfort the Thessalonians about their departed loved ones, 4:13-18.

10. He was prayerful.

(1) He made mention of the Thessalonian believers in his prayers, 1:2.

(2) He prayed earnestly, night and day, that he might see the Thessalonian believers again, 3:10.

(3) He twice offered specific prayer in his letter in behalf of the Thessalonian believers, 3:11-13 and 5:23-24.

Three character traits of the Apostle Paul which greatly influenced the Thessalonians are his love, his faithfulness, and his uprightness.

1. His love

The effect on the Thessalonian believers of Paul's great love for them is seen by the love they had in return for Paul. On his return from Thessalonica, Timothy told the apostle of the believers' happy memories of Paul, of their longing to see him again, and of their steadfastness in the faith in spite of persecution, 3:6-8.

2. His faithfulness

Paul's faithfulness to God in proclaiming the gospel to the Thessalonians in spite of hardship and opposition bore abundant fruit in the salvation of the Thessalonians. These new believers became imitators of Paul and of the Lord in the face of great suffering, welcoming the message with the joy of the Holy Spirit, 1:4-6, 2:13-14. Furthermore, they became a model to all the believers in Greece (Macedonia and Achaia) and even beyond as they spread the Lord's message far and wide, 1:7-8.

Paul was faithful also in giving the new believers (most of whom were undoubtedly Gentiles who had lived under sordid conditions before their conversion) clear instruction on sanctification, 4:1-8. This faithful instruction evidently bore fruit, for in his second epistle to the Thessalonians he found it unnecessary to make any further reference to immorality.

3. His uprightness

In 2:10-12 Paul wrote, "You are witnesses, and so is God, of how holy, righteous and blameless we were among you who believed. For you know that we dealt with each of you as a father deals with his own children, encouraging, comforting and urging you to live lives worthy of God, who calls you into his kingdom and glory."

We see by this that Paul taught the Thessalonian believers not only by precept but also by example—the example of his integrity of character. In 4:1 we see the effect of such exemplary living upon the Thessalonians: "Finally, brothers, we instructed you how to live in order to please God, *as in fact you are living.*"

EXERCISE 7

Without observing the cultural and historical background, and the geographical features of Joshua, you doubtless had difficulty understanding certain parts of it. It is for this reason that we instructed you to make your own map showing the cities that Joshua conquered, the route which he took in his campaign of conquest, and the location of the territory occupied by each of the twelve tribes of Israel. You will now have a much clearer picture of the book of Joshua than ever before.

From Numbers 13 and 14 we see that when the people of Israel came to the borders of the promised land from the south they failed to enter into it. These rebellious Israelites deprived themselves of the blessings which nearly forty years later became the inheritance of their children.

The reading of Numbers 32 should have helped you to understand why two and a half of the tribes of Israel—the tribes of Reuben and Gad, and half of the tribe of Manasseh—were given an inheritance to the east of the Jordan River. It was not the Lord's intention that these tribes occupy a place east of the Jordan. This was a choice of their own, not God's. They thought they knew better than the Lord Himself what was best for them. And when they persisted in their choice God permitted them to have their own way. You can see from reading Joshua 22 that it was not long afterward these two and a half tribes began having difficulty with their inheritances. And many years later these tribes were the first of the tribes of Israel to be carried away into captivity. There are many of us who must admit that we are too much like Manasseh, Reuben, and Gad. Knowing full well God's will for us, we foolishly persist in wanting our own way, only to reap the sad consequences of our willfulness.

By reading Leviticus 18 and Deuteronomy 7:1-6, you have also

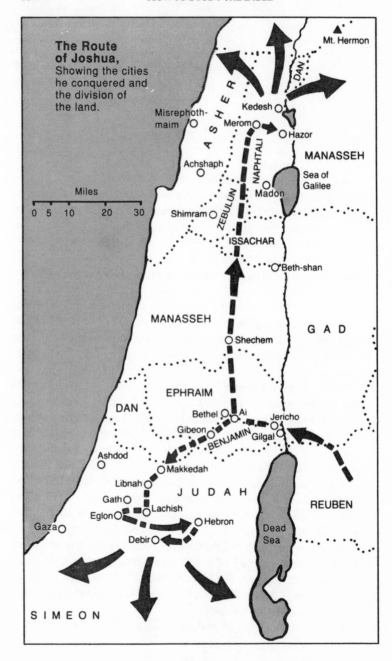

The Route
of Joshua,
Showing the cities
he conquered and
the division of
the land.

Mt. Hermon

Misrephoth-
maim

Kedesh

Merom

Hazor

ASHER

DAN

NAPHTALI

MANASSEH

Achshaph

Sea of
Galilee

Madon

Miles

0 5 10   20   30

Shimram

ZEBULUN

ISSACHAR

Beth-shan

MANASSEH

GAD

Shechem

EPHRAIM

DAN

Bethel   Ai

Jericho

Gibeon

Gilgal

BENJAMIN

Ashdod

Makkedah

Libnah

Gath

JUDAH

Eglon   Lachish

REUBEN

GazaO

Hebron

Dead
Sea

Debir

SIMEON

Figure 17

seen that the people in the land of Canaan were unspeakably vile. Canaan stood at the crossroads of civilization in that age, and the depravity of the Canaanites was infecting the entire world. God's command to Joshua and his people to exterminate the Canaanites was both to punish the Canaanites for their immorality and to prevent it from spreading and corrupting Israel and the rest of the world.

In addition to researching the geography, culture, and history of Joshua, you were asked to construct a synthetic chart on the book of Judges. Compare your chart with mine and see if they correspond (see Figure 18).

The Book of Judges: History of Israel in the Times of the Judges

	1	2	3	4	5	6	7	8	9	10	11	12	13	14	15	16	17	18	19	20	21
	Review of the Times 1-3:4		Incomplete obedience of tribes	Apostasies	Deliverances by Othniel, Ehud, and Shamgar	Deliverances by Deborah and Barak	Song of Deborah and Barak	Calling of Gideon	Deliverance by Gideon	Judgeship under Gideon	Usurpation of Abimelech	Judgeship of Tola and Jair, Deliverance by Jephthah	Judgeship under Jephthah, Elon, and Abdon	Birth of Jephthah, Ibzan,	Deeds of Samson	Deeds of Samson	Downfall of Samson (continued)	Heresy under Samson	Capture of a Levitical priest	Immorality of the Levitical priesthood	War between Israel & Benjamites	Mourning over the Benjamites

	Review of the Times 1-3:4	Judges of the Times 3:5-16	Episodes of the Times 17-21
	Sin of the Israelites	Deliverers of the Israelites	Trouble amidst the Israelites
	Sin	Apostasy	Chaos	Deliverance
	Compromise	Supplication		
	Sin	Chastisement		

Figure 18

EXERCISE 8

1. List all illustrations and implications of God's sovereignty in the book of Jonah. 1:1, 2—God commissions Jonah to deliver His message to Nineveh. 1:4—God sends a storm out on the sea. 1:17—God prepares a great fish to swallow Jonah. 2:10—God commands the fish to release Jonah. 3:1, 2—God commissions Jonah a second time to preach to Nineveh. 3:10—God spares Nineveh from destruction because of their repentence. 4:6—God prepares a vine to provide shade for Jonah. 4:7—God prepares a worm to destroy the plant. 4:8—God prepares a hot east wind which causes Jonah great discomfort. 4:11—God declares His right to spare the city of Nineveh.

2. Codify these examples of God's sovereignty in the book of Jonah.

   a. God exercised His sovereignty over Jonah directly (1:1, 2; 3:1, 2).

   b. God exercised His sovereignty over the objects of His creation: the elements (1:4; 4:8), the creatures of His creation (1:17; 2:10; 4:7), and plant life (4:6).

   c. God exercised His sovereignty over Nineveh (3:10; 4:11).

3. Discover the significance of *sovereignty* when applied to God. The sovereignty of God is the absolute authority which He exercises as Creator over His creation, disposing of His creation in accordance with His own will and exercising His absolute rights over those He has redeemed.

These examples of the exercise of God's sovereignty in the book of Jonah clearly bear this out. First Chronicles 29:11-12 further expresses the concept of sovereignty: "Yours, O LORD, is the greatness and the power and the glory and the majesty and the splendor, for everything in heaven and earth is yours. Yours, O LORD, is the kingdom; you are exalted as head over all. Wealth and honor come from you; you are the ruler of all things. In your hands are strength and power to exalt and give strength to all."

4. Consider in a general way the relationship of Jonah to the sovereignty of God. The instances cited in Part 1 of this exercise show that the Lord is not limited by the things which He has created, nor is He bound by the laws which control the forces of nature. Instead, He is the absolute Master of all that He has made and He puts His creation to use to accomplish His own purposes in any way He pleases.

5. Make a personal application of the truth learned. When I know the will of God concerning a certain matter, my wisest response is to yield fully and unquestioningly to Him. My sovereign God accomplishes His purposes with great ease. Since He has full control of all the elements and all the objects of His creation, there is no limit to what He can do or how He may carry out His designs for my life. God is sovereign over His creation, yet deigns to accomplish His work upon the earth through His faulty servants like you and like me.

EXERCISE 9

We suggested two or three topics which you could use for topical studies in 1 Thessalonians at the conclusion of chapter 9. Those topics are not the only ones to be found in this epistle. For your interest we show below four other topics which can be developed out of the same letter by the Apostle Paul.

They are, practical issues relating to the second coming of Christ; lessons we can learn from the apostle about prayer; Paul's expressions of love to the Thessalonians; and finally, the characteristics of a godly ministry.

Space does not permit us to develop these topics here, but we will show you how to make a topical study on one topic we have mentioned: lessons we can learn about affliction as seen in Paul's first epistle to the Thessalonians.

Step 1. List every occurrence of the topic in the order in which it appears in the book. Although the word *affliction* does not occur in the first epistle to the Thessalonians according to the New International Version, the concept recurs in synonymous terms as follows:

1:6	Suffering
2:2	Suffer
2:9	Hardship
2:14	Suffer
2:15	Drove us out
3:3	Trials
3:4	Persecuted
3:7	Distress
3:7	Persecution

Step 2. Classify the material you have assembled together. There

159

are two ways in which we may group these occurrences of the idea of affliction. First, affliction suffered by the Apostle Paul and his co-laborers. The references in connection with this first category are 2:2, 2:9, 2:15, 3:3, 3:4, and 3:7.

The second category: affliction as it affected the young believers in Thessalonica. The references here are: 1:6, 2:14, 3:3, and 3:4.

Step 3. Discover the meaning of each occurrence of the topic. By the use of extra-biblical sources such as an unabridged concordance, *Vine's Expository Dictionary of New Testament Words,* or a lexicon, we find the following definitions of the terms used for affliction in this epistle. They refer to the King James Version terminology.

Affliction—1:6, 3:3, 3:4, 3:7. Anguish, tribulation, or trouble brought upon an individual by pressure of circumstances or by the antagonism of others.

Suffer—2:2, 2:14. To undergo hardship imposed by an individual from an outside source. This word, *suffer,* is closely related to the term affliction we have just mentioned.

Travail—2:9. Toil, including the idea of sadness or pain.

Persecute—2:15. To pursue relentlessly or to put to flight or to drive out.

Distress—3:7. A troubled concern as that of a parent for his children.

Step 4. Observation of the relationship of the usages of the topic to their contexts. Because of lack of space we shall limit our observations to the afflictions which affected the young believers of Thessalonica and to the context in which these references are found.

1. Though the believers at Thessalonica were mere babes in Christ, the Lord permitted them to undergo trials and suffering of the deepest nature (1:4-6).

2. The Word of God had a large place in the hearts of the Christians before and during their affliction. They were thus fortified for the sufferings which came upon them (1:5, 6; 2:13, 14).

3. The afflictions of the Thessalonians were accompanied by the joy of the Holy Spirit and resulted in the spreading of the Word of God far and wide (1:6-8).

4. Persecution of the Thessalonians did not make them any less willing to suffer for the gospel than the Christians who had been persecuted in Judea (2:14, 15).

5. The first section, containing the first three chapters of the epistle

which refer to the sufferings of the believers, begins and ends with prayer for these believers. In 3:12, 13, Paul petitions that the love of the believers would increase and abound for one another and also for all men.

Step 5. Application of the truths we have learned from our topical study. There are a number of personal applications which we may make, but we shall narrow them here to three pertinent items.

1. I need to spend much time in the Word of God, allowing myself time to read it, meditate upon it, be saturated with it, memorize it, and pray over it so that I may be fortified by it for the day of adversity.

2. I should not fear affliction for the sake of Christ. As the believers in Thessalonica were given the joy of the Holy Spirit and were mightily used for the furtherance of the gospel in the midst of their testings, so also can I be used in any trial I may be called upon to endure for His sake.

3. I need to uphold in prayer fellow Christians who are enduring affliction for Christ, such as those in China and other totalitarian states. I need to pray that their hearts might be knit together in love so that in the midst of their trials, they may comfort and strengthen one another in the grace of Christ.

EXERCISE 10

1. Derive two principles for each of the first seven verses of 1 Thessalonians 1.

Verse 1—The work of God prospers where the servant of the Lord works with other believers as a team. The experience of the peace of God is always preceded by the experience of the grace of God.

Verse 2—Intercession is an important part of the ministry of prayer. Giving thanks to God for our fellow believers is just as vital as praying for them.

Verse 3— Believers can possess the three graces of the Christian life: faith, love, and hope. Christians who possess the cardinal graces of the Christian life become a source of joy to their spiritual fathers.

Verse 4—Christians are vitally related as brothers to one another. We are chosen by God to be members of one spiritual family.

Verse 5—The good news of the Gospel produces blessed results when it is preached in the power of the Holy Spirit. Powerful preaching and holy living go together.

Verse 6—The ultimate success of our preaching is seen in the degree to which men follow the Lord. The joy of the Holy Spirit can supersede any suffering we may have to endure for our faith.

Verse 7—An overcoming Christian becomes a noble example to other believers. A vital testimony for Christ can have a widespread influence.

2. Write a comprehensive principle for each of the two main divisions of 1 Thessalonians.

Chapters 1-3: We will win the confidence of our brothers in Christ by manifesting a personal interest in them.

Chapters 4-5: Right teaching is necessary for right living.

3. Write a comprehensive principle covering the entire epistle of 1 Thessalonians in the light of its contents and background. The sec-

ond coming of Christ is the great hope of the church under trial.

4. Prepare a comprehensive principle for each of the four main divisions in the book of Joshua.

Chapters 1-5:12: Adequate preparation is essential for success in spiritual conflict.

Chapters 5:13-12: We are assured of victory when we meet God's conditions for fighting the spiritual warfare.

Chapters 13-22: We can experience spiritual blessings only as we appropriate them by faith.

Chapters 23-24: It is God's desire that we retain the blessings He has given to us.

5. Prepare a comprehensive principle covering the entire book of Joshua in the light of its contents and background. Every believer is expected to enter into possession of his spiritual possessions in Christ.

EXERCISE 11

The bronze snake set up by Moses in the wilderness, as recorded in Numbers 21:4-9 was a type of Christ in the following respects:

1. In the need for it.
   (1) It was set up for people who had sinned. Christ was offered up for the sins of many, Romans 5:8, Hebrews 9:27-28.
   (2) It was set up for those who were dying because they had sinned. Christ was hung upon the cross because men were doomed to spiritual death as a result of sin, Romans 5:6-8.
   (3) It was set up for those who had no other means of escape from death. Christ hung on Calvary's cross because there was no other way for man to escape spiritual death, John 14:6, 3:14-15, Acts 4:12.

2. In the provision of it.
   (1) It was divinely appointed. It was not thought of or provided by man, but by God. The salvation we have as a result of Christ's sacrifice on the cross is entirely of God's own doing, not man's, Romans 5:21, John 3:16-17.
   (2) It was made like a snake, the very thing which produced the sting of death. "The sting of death is sin," 1 Corinthians 15:56, but "God made him who had no sin to be sin for us," 2 Corinthians 5:21.
   (3) It was the only means of escape from death. In the same way, Christ's work on the cross is the only means of escape from eternal death, John 5:24, 14:6, Acts 4:12.

3. In the adequacy of it.

(1) It could be seen by all who had been bitten; it was available to everyone. Christ declared, "I, when I am lifted up from the earth, will draw all men to myself" (John 12:32), and because He was lifted up on the cross, His atoning work is now available to every guilty sinner, John 3:14-15.

(2) It was sufficient for the need of every one who had been bitten. Christ's death on the cross is sufficient for the need of every sinner, no matter what his condition may be, John 3:16-17, 6:37.

4. In the efficacy of it.

(1) It was accompanied by a promise to anyone who had been bitten that he would live by looking at the bronze snake. By the work of Christ on the cross, all who look to Christ for salvation from sin are assured of eternal life, John 3:14-15, Romans 6:23.

(2) It was effective for every individual who took the Lord at His Word concerning the bronze snake. In the same way, eternal life becomes the possession of each individual who personally takes God at His Word concerning salvation from sin through the work of Christ on the cross, John 3:36, 5:24; Acts 10:43, 13:38-39.

What main truth do we learn from an examination of the bronze snake as a type of Christ? Simply this—we are saved from sin solely by believing in what Christ did for us at Calvary.

There is life in a look at the crucified One,
There is life at this moment for thee.
Then look, sinner, look unto Him and be saved,
Unto Him who was nailed to the tree.

Recommended Source Books for Research in Bible Study

Meanings of Words
(No Knowledge of Greek or Hebrew Necessary)

Old Testament

1. Unger, Merrill F.; and White, William Jr. *Nelson's Expository Dictionary of the Old Testament*. Nashville, Tennessee: Thomas Nelson, 1980.

   For those who do not read Hebrew, this is probably the most helpful book giving meanings of Hebrew words. It makes an excellent companion volume to *Vine's Expository Dictionary of New Testament Words*.

2. Vine, W.E. *An Expository Dictionary of Old Testament Words*. Old Tappan, New Jersey: Fleming H. Revell Company, 1978.

   Because of Vine's death, this work is incomplete. What there is, however, is helpful.

3. Wilson, William. *Wilson's Old Testament Word Studies*. Grand Rapids, Michigan: Kregel Publications.

   Though the English reader can use this profitably, it is best used with some knowledge of Hebrew.

New Testament

1. Vine, W.E. *An Expository Dictionary of New Testament Words*.

   Now available from several publishers, this book gives the meanings of Greek words, listing them alphabetically by their English translations.

Meanings of Words
(Some Knowledge of Greek or Hebrew Necessary)

Old Testament

1. Brown, F.; Driver, S. R.; and Briggs, C.A. *A Hebrew Lexicon of the Old Testament*. New York: Oxford University Press.

   This is the most authoritative lexicon of biblical Hebrew available today in English.

2. Davidson, Benjamin. *Analytical Hebrew and Chaldee Lexicon*. Grand Rapids, Michigan: Zondervan Publishing House.

   Gives parts of speech for words in the Hebrew Old Testament.

3. Holladay, William L. *A Concise Hebrew and Aramaic Lexicon of the Old Testament*. Grand Rapids, Michigan: Wm. B. Eerdmans Publishing Co., 1971.

   Although not as thorough as Brown, Driver, and Briggs, it presents a more concise, affordable alternative to the larger work.

New Testament

1. Arndt, W. F.; and Gingrich, F. W. *A Greek-English Lexicon of the New Testament*. Chicago: University of Chicago Press.

   This is the most authoritative lexicon of New Testament Greek available today in English.

2. Gingrich, F. W. *Shorter Lexicon of the Greek New Testament*. Chicago: University of Chicago Press, 1957.

   A conveniently sized lexicon which can be carried with your New Testament.

3. Lampe, G. W. H. *Patristic Greek Lexicon*. New York: Oxford University Press.

   This is the authoritative lexicon for Patristic (sacred post-New Testament) Greek.

4. Liddell, H. G.; and Scott, R. *Greek-English Lexicon*. New York: Oxford University Press, 1940.

   This is the authoritative lexicon for classical Greek.

5. Thayer, Joseph H. *Greek-English Lexicon of the New Testament.*
   This was once the standard. It is still quite useful, though not on a par with Arndt and Gingrich.

6. _____ . *Analytical Greek Lexicon.* Grand Rapids, Michigan: Zondervan Publishing House.
   This book gives the parts of speech for words in the Greek New Testament.

Concordances

Of English Translations: King James Version

1. Cruden, Alexander. *Cruden's Complete Concordance.*
   Though not exhaustive, this concordance meets the needs of most Bible students.

2. Strong, James. *Strong's Exhaustive Concordance of the Bible.*
   Every occurrence of every word in the KJV is listed.

3. Young, Robert. *Analytical Concordance to the Bible.*
   This book and Strong's are the two most complete for the KJV.

Of English Translations: Revised Standard Version

1. Morrison, Clinton. *An Analytical Concordance to the Revised Standard Version of the New Testament.* Philadelphia: Westminster Press.

2. *Nelson's Complete Concordance of the Revised Standard Version,* 2nd ed. Nashville: Thomas Nelson, Inc.

Of English Translations: New American Standard Bible

1. Thomas, Robert. *New American Standard Exhaustive Concordance to the Bible.* Nashville: A. J. Holman Co., 1981.

Of English Translations: New International Version

1. Goodrick, E. W.; and Kohlenberger, J. R. *NIV Complete Concordance*. Grand Rapids, Michigan: Zondervan Publishing House, 1981.

Other English Translations

1. Darton, Michael. *Modern Concordance to the New Testament*. Garden City, New York: Doubleday & Co., Inc., 1976.
   This concordance is designed to be used with six different English versions.

Of the Hebrew Old Testament

1. Lisowsky, Gerhard. *Koncordanz zum Hebraischen Alten Testament*. Available through the American Bible Society.
   This book lists every occurrence of the Hebrew word, along with its context in the Hebrew Old Testament. What's not in Hebrew in this volume is in German.

2. Wigram, George. *Englishman's Hebrew and Chaldee Concordance*. Grand Rapids, Michigan: Zondervan Publishing House.
   This book lists every occurrence of the Hebrew word, along with its context in the King James Version.

Of the Greek New Testament

1. Moulton, J. H.; and Geden, G. *Concordance to the Greek New Testament*. Grand Rapids, Michigan: Kregel Publications.
   This book lists every occurrence of the Greek word, along with its context in the Greek New Testament.

2. Wigram, George. *Englishman's Greek Concordance of the New Testament*. Grand Rapids, Michigan: Zondervan Publishing House.
   This book lists every occurrence of the Greek word, along with its context in the King James Version.

Word Studies

Old Testament

1. Botterweck, G. J.; and Ringgren, H. *Theological Dictionary of the Old Testament*. Grand Rapids, Michigan: Wm. B. Eerdmans Publishing Co.

   This set of twelve (projected) volumes, though somewhat technical, in an authoritative source of information on Hebrew words.

2. Harris, R.; Archer, Gleason L.; and Waltke, Bruce K. *Theological Wordbook of the Old Testament*. Chicago: Moody Press, 1981.

   Though far more concise and limited than the *Theological Dictionary of the Old Testament,* it is probably more usable by the average Bible student, especially those who also use Strong's Concordance, to which this two-volume set is keyed.

New Testament

1. Barclay, William. *New Testament Words*. Philadelphia: Westminster Press, 1974.

   This little book has always fascinating and usually (but not always) accurate information about many New Testament words.

2. Brown, Colin. *Dictionary of New Testament Theology*. Grand Rapids, Michigan: Zondervan Publishing House, 1976.

   This three-volume set does much of what Kittel does, but in a more concise and economical manner.

3. Bullinger, E. W. *Figures of Speech Used in the Bible*. Grand Rapids, Michigan: Baker Book House, 1968.

   This book describes scores of literary devices used in the Bible, giving examples of them.

4. Earle, Ralph. *Word Meanings in the New Testament*. Kansas City, Missouri: Beacon Hill Press.

   This is a fairly simple, easy-to-read set. Earle leans heavily on the work of others. Useful, if not very original.

5. Kittel, Gerhard. *Theological Dictionary of the New Testament*. Grand Rapids, Michigan: Wm. B. Eerdmans Publishing Co., 1964-76.

This ten-volume set is a standard of scholarship on Greek words of theological significance.

6. Moulton, J. H.; and Milligan, George. *The Vocabulary of the Greek New Testament*. Grand Rapids, Michigan: Wm. B. Eerdmans Publishing Co., 1930.

    This book illustrates how words in the New Testament were used in non-Biblical sources.

7. Robertson, A. T. *Word Pictures in the New Testament*. Nashville: Broadman Press, 1943.

    This six volume set is more technical and more useful than Wuest's or Vincent's.

8. Vincent, M. R. *Word Studies in the New Testament*. Grand Rapids, Michigan: Wm. B. Eerdmans Publishing Co., 1957.

    This work is not as detailed as Robertson's, but is still quite useful. It provides a commentary on the New Testament.

9. Wuest, Kenneth. *Word Studies in the Greek New Testament*. Grand Rapids, Michigan: Wm. B. Eerdmans Publishing Co.

    Although poorly edited and indexed, this set is nevertheless quite helpful. It provides a commentary on many books of the New Testament.

Bible Dictionaries and Encyclopedias

One Volume Dictionaries

1. Bryant, Alton. *New Compact Bible Dictionary*. Grand Rapids, Michigan: Zondervan Publishing House, 1967.

    Although this is not nearly as extensive as the others listed here, it is the best of the small Bible dictionaries. A paperback is available at a very reasonable price.

2. Douglas, J. D. *New Bible Dictionary*. Grand Rapids, Michigan: Wm. B. Eerdmans Publishing Co., 1962.

    Although this is out of print, it is still the finest single-volume Bible dictionary around.

3. Tenney, Merrill C. *Zondervan Pictorial Bible Dictionary*. Grand

Rapids, Michigan: Zondervan Publishing House, 1969.

Probably the best one volume Bible dictionary still in print. More than half the pages have some illustration on them.

4. Unger, Merrill F. *Unger's Bible Dictionary*. Chicago: Moody Press, 1957.

This very popular work is very helpful, but could use revision in some articles.

Multi-volume Encyclopedias

1. Bromiley, Geoffrey W. *International Standard Bible Encyclopedia*, rev. ed. Grand Rapids, Michigan: Wm. B. Eerdmans Publishing Co., 1988.

This four-volume work is among the finest available.

2. Buttrick, George Arthur. *Interpreter's Dictionary of the Bible*. Nashville: Abingdon Press, 1962.

This four-volume set, plus the Supplementary volume (1976), which updates the set, is an excellent one, especially in matters of geography, history, and culture. It is liberal in theology.

3. Douglas, J. D. *Illustrated Bible Dictionary*. Wheaton, Illinois: Tyndale House Publishers, 1981.

The text is a revision of the *New Bible Dictionary*. The illustrations are lavish, well chosen, and helpful. This is a lovely three-volume set.

4. Orr, James. *International Standard Bible Encyclopedia*. Grand Rapids, Michigan: Wm. B. Eerdmans Publishing Co., 1915.

This work was the standard for years, and many of its articles are still unsurpassed. However, because it is dated, it has now been fully revised.

5. Pfeiffer, C. F.; Vos, H. F.; and Rea, John. *Wycliffe Bible Encyclopedia*. Chicago: Moody Press, 1975.

A fine two-volume set that is concise, but complete.

6. Tenney, Merrill C. *Zondervan Pictorial Bible Encyclopedia*. Grand Rapids, Michigan: Zondervan Publishing House, 1974.

This five-volume set is to be ranked at or near the top.

Bible Handbooks

1. Alexander, David; and Alexander, Pat. *Eerdman's Handbook to the Bible*. Grand Rapids, Michigan: Wm. B. Eerdmans Publishing Co., 1973.

   This is the best of the Bible handbooks, both in terms of text and its lovely, instructive illustrations.

2. Beers, V. Gilbert. *Victor Handbook of Bible Knowledge*. Wheaton, Illinois: Victor Books, 1981.

   This is a family book giving background and exposition of most major events in scripture, arranged in biblical order. The illustrations appeal to young and old alike.

3. Halley, Henry H. *Halley's Bible Handbook*. Grand Rapids, Michigan; Zondervan Publishing House.

4. Unger, Merrill F. *Unger's Bible Handbook*. Chicago: Moody Press, 1966.

   Unger's and Halley's are very similar. It is amazing how much information can be packed into such small volumes. Either book provides an economical alternative to Eerdman's.

Bible Atlases

1. Aharoni, Y.; and Avi-Yonah, M. *Macmillan Bible Atlas*, rev. ed. New York: Macmillan Publishing Co., Inc., 1977.

   This is generally considered the best. It has many (264) maps which portray virtually every biblical event that can be depicted cartographically.

2. Frank, Harry Thomas. *Hammond's Atlas of the Bible Lands*. Wheaton, Illinois: Scripture Press, 1977.

   A reasonably priced paperback atlas with maps which do a better than average job of showing topography.

3. May, Herbert G. *Oxford Bible Atlas*. New York: Oxford University Press, 1974.

   This has an excellent index to the maps.

4. Monson, J. *Student Map Manual: Historical Geography of the Bible Lands*. Grand Rapids, Michigan: Zondervan Publishing House, 1979.

   Has the most detailed maps of these Bible atlases, along with excellent indexes, cross-references, and space for notes. Uses the biblical eastward orientation. Limited to Palestine.

5. Wright. G. E.; and Filson, Floyd V. *Westminster Historical Atlas to the Bible*. Philadelphia: Westminster Press, 1956.

   Very large maps, with great detail—possibly too cluttered.

6. *Compact Bible Atlas with Gazetteer*. Grand Rapids, Michigan: Baker Book House, 1979.

   Because of its small size, it is most convenient to carry. Has the same maps as the Hammond's, but a better index.

Bible Introduction

Old Testament

1. Archer, Gleason. *Survey of Old Testament Introduction*. Chicago: Moody Press, 1973.

   A good standard textbook. It is semi-technical, perhaps too difficult for some beginners.

2. Bullock, C. Hassel. *An Introduction to the Old Testament Poetic Books*. Chicago: Moody Press, 1979.

   A very fine work on the books of this particular literary genre. Of medium difficulty.

3. Freeman, Hobart E. *An Introduction to the Old Testament Prophets*. Chicago: Moody Press.

   An excellent work on these biblical books. This makes a good companion volume to Bullock's work.

4. Harrison, R. K. *Introduction to the Old Testament*. Grand Rapids, Michigan: Wm. B. Eerdmans Publishing Co., 1969.

   Though excellent, this work is quite technical, and probably not the best for beginners.

5. Jensen, Irving C. *Jensen's Survey of the Old Testament*. Chicago:

Moody Press, 1978.

This work makes excellent use of charts and a basic text. It is very good for a basic Old Testament introduction and survey.

6. Mears, Henrietta. *What the Bible Is All About*. Ventura, California: Gospel Light Publications, 1953.

This is a very simple volume, but can be of help to the beginning Bible student. It covers both Old and New Testament.

7. Unger, Merrill F. *Introductory Guide to the Old Testament*. Grand Rapids, Michigan: Zondervan Publishing House, 1951.

Complete, but not too technical. Very good for beginners.

8. Young, Edward J. *Introduction to the Old Testament*. Grand Rapids, Michigan: Wm. B. Eerdmans Publishing Co., 1949.

A good standard textbook.

New Testament

1. Foulkes, Francis. *Pocket Guide to the New Testament*. Downers Grove, Illinois: InterVarsity Press, 1978.

A concise and very basic work. Includes study questions, topics for further study, and a brief bibliography.

2. Guthrie, Donald. *New Testament Introduction*. Downers Grove, Illinois: InterVarsity Press, 1970.

This volume, though perhaps too technical for some beginners, is probably the finest New Testament introduction.

3. Harrison, Everett F. *Introduction to the New Testament*. Grand Rapids, Michigan: Wm. B. Eerdmans Publishing Co., 1964.

A standard college-level text with good general New Testament introductory material, as well as individual book introductions.

4. Hiebert, D. Edmond. *Introduction to the New Testament,* 3 vol. Chicago: Moody Press, 1977.

Volume 1, The Gospels and Acts; Volume 2, The Pauline Epistles; Volume 3, The Non-Pauline Epistles and Revelation. This is an excellent set, covering the more technical introductory problems in a clear, non-technical manner. The work includes fine bibliographies on each biblical book.

5. Jensen, Irving L. *Jensen's Survey of the New Testament*. Chicago: Moody Press, 1981.

This work, like its Old Testament companion, is concise and easy to use, with excellent charts.

Bible Geography and History

1. Adams, J. McKee. *Biblical Backgrounds*. Nashville: Broadman Press, 1965.

   More concise than Baly, Pfeiffer, or Smith, this book gives excellent historical information on many biblical areas, including those outside of Palestine.

2. Baly, Denis. *Geography of the Bible*. New York: Harper & Row, 1974.

   Though some history is given, the emphasis is on the geography and climate. In these areas the book is unsurpassed. Limited to Palestine.

3. Bright, John. *A History of Israel*. Philadelphia: Westminster Press, 1972.

   One of the finest Old Testament histories available, despite its acceptance of several liberal critical views.

4. Davis, John J.; and Whitcomb, John C. *A History of Israel: From Conquest to Exile*. Grand Rapids, Michigan: Baker Book House, 1980.

   Originally published as three paperback volumes, this work covers the Old Testament period with a strong emphasis on the historical and archaeological backgrounds of that period.

5. Pfeiffer, Charles R.; and Vos, Howard F. *Wycliffe Historical Geography of Bible Lands*. Chicago: Moody Press, 1967.

   A most excellent work giving information for not only Palestine, but all Old and New Testament lands of biblical significance. Well-written in non-technical language.

6. Smith, George Adam. *Historical Geography of the Holy Land*. Grand Rapids, Michigan: Kregel Publications.

   A classic in this field, still considered by some to be the finest of its kind ever done.

7. Wood, Leon. *A Survey of Israel's History*. Grand Rapids, Michigan: Zondervan Publishing House, 1970.
   This is a good book introducing the history of Israel in Old Testament times.

Bible Manners and Customs

1. Alexander, Patricia, ed. *Eerdman's Family Encyclopedia of the Bible*. Grand Rapids, Michigan: Wm. B. Eerdmans Publishing Co., 1978.
   This beautiful volume gives much information on manners and customs in the most attractive and interesting format available. You can well leave this on your coffee table when not in use.

2. Bouquet, A. C. *Everyday Life in New Testament Times*. New York: Charles Scribner's Sons, 1953.
   Very excellent volume, somewhat technical, on the physical anthropology of New Testament times.

3. de Vaux, Roland. *Ancient Israel*. New York: McGraw-Hill Book Co., 1965. Volume 1, Social Institutions; Volume 2, Religious Institutions.
   This two-volume set is very complete and scholarly. It may be the most thorough treatment of the subject available at a reasonable price.

4. Heaton, Eric W. *Everyday Life in Old Testament Times*. New York: Charles Scribner's Sons, 1977.
   Companion to Bouquet. Very good information, but possibly more technical than some would need.

5. Miller, Madeleine S.; and Miller, J. Lane. *Harper's Encyclopedia of Bible Life*. New York: Harper & Row, 1978.
   More complete than Wight, but might be a little wordy. Very helpful indexes, as well as suggestions for further reading.

6. Packer, J. I.; Tenney, Merrill C.; and White, William Jr. *The Bible Almanac*. Nashville: Thomas Nelson, Inc., 1980.
   This is a large volume packed with information on this subject.

Not only is the text good, but the illustrations and index are very useful.

7. Wight, Fred H. *Manners and Customs of Bible Lands*. Chicago: Moody Press, 1953.

    This book deals topically with manners and customs in a simple, well-written manner.

8. Wright, G. Ernest, ed. *Great People of the Bible and How They Lived*. New York: Reader's Digest Association, 1974.

    This large and lavish volume has much good information on manners and customs, though Bible history seems to be its focus.

9. Specific articles on various topics (e.g. dress, houses, etc.) in any good Bible dictionary.

Archaeology

1. Kitchen, D. A. *The Bible in Its World*. Downers Grove, Illinois: InterVarsity Press, 1977.

    Kitchen ably brings archaeology to bear upon the various periods of Bible history.

2. Lewis, Jack P. *Archaeological Backgrounds to Bible People*. Grand Rapids, Michigan: Baker Book House, 1971.

    An informative book of what archaeology has contributed to the history of various persons mentioned in Scripture. Originally titled *Historical Backgrounds of Bible History*.

3. Pfeiffer, Charles F. *The Biblical World: A Dictionary of Biblical Archaeology*. Grand Rapids, Michigan: Baker Book House, 1964.

    This volume alphabetically lists articles dealing with various aspects of biblical archaeology: places, persons, things, etc. An easy-to-use reference volume.

4. Schoville, Keith N. *Biblical Archaeology in Focus*. Grand Rapids, Michigan: Baker Book House.

    This book does a fine job of covering both the methods and the findings of biblical archaeology.

5. Unger, Merrill F. *Archaeology and the Old Testament*. Chicago:

Moody Press: 1954.

This has much helpful information on the subject, but it could use some updating now. There is only a small section dealing with the role of biblical archaeology.

6. _____ . *Archaeology of the New Testament*. Chicago: Moody Press, 1962.

A companion to his work on the Old Testament. It also could use some updating.

7. Vos, Howard F. *Archaeology in Bible Lands*. Chicago: Moody Press, 1977.

An excellent and complete text. The first 100 pages deal with the nature of biblical archaeology and the last 300 pages with a regional survey of the findings of archaeology.

8. _____ . *Beginnings in Bible Archaeology*. Chicago: Moody Press, 1956.

A good little introduction to the subject, with the emphasis on the discipline of biblical archaeology more than the findings of archaeology.

Commentaries

One Volume

1. Church, Leslie F., ed. *Matthew Henry's Commentary on the Whole Bible*. Grand Rapids, Michigan: Zondervan Publishing House, 1961.

If you want an inspirational, devotional commentary in one volume, this is probably the best. But if you want something that explains the meaning of the text, get something else.

2. Guthrie, D.; Moyer, J. A.; Stibbs, A. M.; and Wiseman, D. J. *The New Bible Commentary,* rev. ed. Grand Rapids, Michigan: Wm. B. Eerdmans Publishing Co., 1970.

Very helpful whole Bible commentary, which tends to be a bit more synthetic in its approach than the Wycliffe.

3. Howley, G. C. D.; Bruce, F. F.; and Ellison, H. L. *The New*

Layman's Bible Commentary. Grand Rapids, Michigan: Zondervan Publishing House, 1979.

May be the best of this group. Has helpful, essentially verse-by-verse commentary, but also includes numerous introductory and background articles which are, for the most part, very good.

4. Pfeiffer, Charles F.; and Harrison, Everett F. *Wycliffe Bible Commentary*. Chicago: Moody Press, 1962.

A helpful expository commentary.

Sets or Series

1. Barclay, William. *Daily Study Bible*. Philadelphia: Westminster Press.

This eighteen-volume set on the New Testament is one of the most fascinating, due to the author's writing skill. There is also much valuable information in it, although the conservative reader will not always find Barclay's theology to his liking.

2. Bruce, F. F., gen. ed. *New International Commentary on the New Testament*. Grand Rapids, Michigan: Wm. B. Eerdmans Publishing Co.

Though somewhat technical, this series is so excellent that even the beginner should be aware of it. It is hard to find a more consistant level of high quality than in this eighteen-volume set.

3. Ellicott, Charles John. *Ellicott's Commentary on the Whole Bible*. Grand Rapids, Michigan: Zondervan Publishing House.

This set, first published in the last century, is still an insightful and reverential set of commentaries.

4. Gaebelein, Frank E., gen. ed. *The Expositor's Bible Commentary*. Grand Rapids, Michigan: Zondervan Publishing House.

This set (projected at twelve volumes) is an excellent one, based on the text of the NIV. The passages are dealt with in a clear expositional manner, with critical notes separate for more advanced readers.

5. Harrison, R. K., gen. ed. *New International Commentary on the Old Testament*. Grand Rapids, Michigan: Wm. B. Eerdmans Publishing Co.

This is the companion series to the *New International Commen-*

tary on the New Testament, and is also of the same high level of excellence.

6. Jamieson, R.; Faussett, A. R.; and Brown, D. *A Commentary: Critical, Experimental, and Practical.* Grand Rapids, Michigan: Wm. B. Eerdmans Publishing House.

    This set was first published in the 1800s, but it is also one of the better sets. A bit more technical than Ellicott.

7. Lange, Joseph P. *Commentary on the Holy Scriptures.* Grand Rapids, Michigan: Zondervan Publishing House.

    This unique twelve-volume set is geared for every need and every level of reader. Each section of scripture is handled three separate times, first critically and exegetically, then doctrinally, and finally, practically. It dates from the 1800s.

8. Tasker, R. V. G., gen. ed. *Tyndale New Testament Commentary Series.* Grand Rapids, Michigan: Wm. B. Eerdmans Publishing Co.

    This twenty-volume paperback series is perhaps the best buy on a set of New Testament commentaries. A high level of conservative scholarship is maintained throughout the series.

9. Wiseman, D. J., gen. ed. *Tyndale Old Testament Commentaries.* Downers Grove, Illinois: InterVarsity Press.

    This series (projected at twenty-four volumes) is comparable to the series by the same name on the New Testament. Most volumes are now available, and thus far the series is very good.

10. *Everyman's Bible Commentaries.* Chicago: Moody Press.

    This series of small paperbacks (approximately forty) covers most books in the Bible. They are very basic and simple, but by top-notch scholars with excellent credentials.

Commentaries on Specific Books of the Bible

Quite often many of the finest commentaries are individual works on specific books of the Bible. Rather than list these here, we will suggest several sources of information about them.

• Many of the works previously cited include excellent bibliographies, some annotated. These can be of great help.

- Often a Christian leader (pastor, elder, teacher, etc.) will be able to recommend books that will match your area of interest with your level of scholastic ability.

- There are several books that list commentaries on the various books of the Bible, as well as other types of biblical research books. Such lists (as with this list) will tend to include the author's favorites and exclude those he does not prefer. They will also tend to be geared for a higher scholastic level than that of many readers of this book (often the seminarian). Nevertheless, they are quite useful, and we list several here.

1. Barber, Cyril J. *The Minister's Library*. Grand Rapids, Michigan: Baker Book House, 1974.

    This is the largest and most complete work of this kind done by a conservative. The annotations are brief but helpful. Every few years the author issues a *Periodic Supplement,* which brings the work up to date.

2. Barker, Kenneth L.; and Waltke, Bruce K. *Bibliography for Old Testament Exposition and Exegesis.* Dallas, Texas: Dallas Theological Seminary, 1975.

    Although there are no annotations, the compilors indicate by an asterisk what they consider most essential to the seminarian's library.

3. Goldingay, John. *Old Testament Commentary Survey*. Downers Grove, Illinois: InterVarsity Press, 1977.

    Although this book can be quite helpful, it lists so many out of print books that it is at times frustrating.

4. Johnson, S. Lewis, Jr. *Bibliography for New Testament Exegesis and Exposition*. Dallas, Texas: Dallas Theological Seminary.

    This work is geared more for the expositor than the exegete, and it has very brief comments on each title.

5. Thiselton, Anthony C. *New Testament Commentary Survey,* rev. by Don Carson. Downers Grove, Illinois: Inter-Varsity Press, 1977.

    The companion volume to Goldingay. Both works lean toward rather technical commentaries.

Topical Indexes

1. Joy, Charles. R. *Harper's Topical Concordance*. New York: Harper & Row, 1976.

   This volume is quite similar to Holman's. However, because it is considerably more expensive, the Holman Concordance is probably the better choice.

2. Nave, Orville J. *Nave's Topical Bible*. Chicago: Moody Press, 1975.

   Lists over 20,000 topics or subtopics, with over 100,000 scripture references. This is the most popular of the "topical Bibles."

3. Viening, Edward, ed. *Zondervan Topical Bible*. Grand Rapids, Michigan: Zondervan Publishing House, 1969.

   About 21,000 topics and subtopics list over 100,000 scripture references. This is very similar to Nave's, both in design and in completeness.

4. Wharton, Gary. *The New Compact Topical Bible*. Grand Rapids, Michigan: Zondervan Publishing House, 1972.

   If you don't mind flipping the pages of your Bible to read the references, this is the book to get. Though about one-third the size (and price) of *Nave's* or *Zondervan's*, it actually has more references in it than either of those volumes. Over 25,000 subtopics and well over 100,000 references are included.

5. *Holman Topical Concordance*. Nashville: A. J. Holman Co., 1973.

   This book lists references according to subject, with each subject having subtopics in outline form.